GIVE THEM A REAL SCARE THIS HALLOWEEN

A GUIDE TO SCARING TRICK-OR-TREATERS AND HAUNTING YOUR HOUSE, YARD OR PARTY

WRITTEN & ILLUSTRATED BY

JOSEPH PFEIFFER

EDITED BY

RANDOLPH METZ

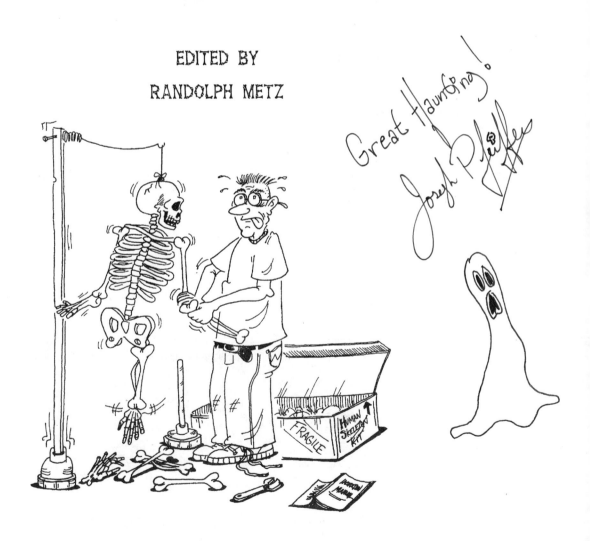

Chessmore Publishing Company   Chapel Hill, NC © 1997

Published by:

Chessmore Publishing Company
PO Box 16572
Chapel Hill, NC 27516-6572
http://chessmorepublishing.com

This book is available at special discounts when purchased in bulk for premiums and sales promotions. Special editions can also be created to specification. Contact the special sales director at the address above. Direct inquiries and/or orders to the above address.

Library of Congress # 97-92452
ISBN 0-9659772-0-X

Short Cut...

DISCLAIMER

This book in no way condones illegal or unethical activity! It is your responsibility to determine the legality of your actions. Further, because we have no control over the workmanship, materials, tools, methods, or testing procedures employed, we hereby disclaim any responsibility for consequences resulting from the fabrication or compounding of any item described in this book. Neither the author nor the publisher assumes any responsibility for the use or misuse of information contained in this book.

This publication is designed to provide accurate and authoritative information with regard to the subject matter covered. It is sold with the understanding that the publisher is not engaged in rendering legal, accounting, or other professional advice. If legal advice or other expert assistance is required, seek the services of a qualified professional.

We at no time recommend the dropping of objects, boiling liquids, or dead bodies on unsuspecting trick-or-treaters. Nor do we recommend the use of pyrotechnics, electric shock, hypnotism, or deep yard pits as a means of satisfying some sadistic and cruel sense of humor. We plan to save these for future editions to ensure you master the basics first, before advancing.

This book is sold for informational purposes only!

CERTIFICATE OF HAUNTMANSHIP

This certifies that

_____

has successfully completed the

Jr. Haunt Master
Basic Training Course

Signature *Joseph Pfeiffer*   Date *2/30/98*

Signature *Berry U. Alive*   Date *2/30/98*

Signature   Date

Haunters Seal of Fright

☠☠☠☠☠☠☠**VALIDATION CHECK LIST**☠☠☠☠☠☠☠☠☠☠☠

You must have each section checked off to earn your certificate

GIVE THEM A REAL SCARE THIS HALLOWEEN

A GUIDE TO SCARING TRICK-OR-TREATERS AND HAUNTING YOUR HOUSE, YARD, OR PARTY

☠☠☠☠☠☠☠☠☠☠☠☠☠ Table of Contents ☠☠☠☠☠☠☠☠☠☠☠☠☠

READ THIS FIRST TO GET STARTED

WHY BUY THIS BOOK?

So, you've decided to get a little more serious about having fun on Halloween this year. Well, we think this book is just what you'll  need. Most people were brought up to know that *no one* reads the book's introduction, forward, preface, or what ever other glitzy name the author gives it. This section is often used as filler, or for the authors to brag about their talents and accomplishments. Since we really have none, we'll get right to the point. That is, to explain how you can earn a newfound level of respect in your neighborhood through fear and intimidation, and have fun doing so.

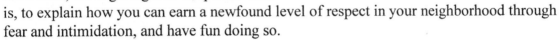

The objectives we set in writing this book were twofold. First, to provide you important tools needed to plan any great haunt, exposure to what others have done to frighten trick-or-treaters, scare haunted house patrons, or shake up party goers. Secondly, we wanted to help you develop a distorted imagination allowing you to design your own new and original effects to keep the belief in poltergeists alive.

Just don't blame us if your friends notice a subtle shift in your personality. If we hadn't showed up, some other bad influence would have entered into your life sooner or later. One thing we know for sure, it will be a whole lot more fun handing out candy this year, so read on, and take notes. There may be a test at the end.

The Halloween holiday has become the second largest merchandising holiday over the past ten years. This explains all the specialty shops that crop up in September and October in otherwise vacant retail space selling a wide variety of Halloween props, costumes, masks, and decorations. Haunted attractions in general have become a huge market.

So how does all this effect you? Well my friend, if you want to experience the type of sheer unbridled mischief and fun you had as a kid, then read on. This book was written for three types of readers, the Halloween enthusiast who wants to learn new ways to enjoy the holiday, the curious, and for those who bought this book looking for a few laughs. Regardless of your reasons, by the time you finish, we bet that you'll never walk by another latex mask display again without stopping for at least a quick look. But first, we have a little groundwork to cover before we get started.

We share parents' concerns over what's suitable or appropriate for our kids these days. You don't *have* to get gross to shock a trick or treater, so if body parts are something you'd prefer to see left in the biology lab, take heart (excuse the expression), there are still a wide variety of options to choose from. Though we include some gross stuff, we provide hundreds of other ways to frighten kids too. A spooky layout for your Halloween yard exhibit can actually return more candy from rapidly retreating trick-or-treaters than is handed out. Our philosophy is that trick-or-treaters should work for their candy. Sure, not using body parts may leave you without "a leg to stand on," or keep you from getting "a-head" of the other neighbors. But, whoever said two heads are better than one probably never had to pay the orthodontist's bills.

Reading this book provides you with a unique opportunity. You'll be able to jump around to any of the chapters in the book without following the traditional and rigid sequential chapter *reading laws* that govern most literature throughout the Western Hemisphere. Yes, we're talking about the freedom to scan and browse that you probably haven't experienced since you put down your last MAD® magazine.

Reward

WANTED, EXCEPTIONAL ILLUSIONS OR EFFECTS USED TO SCARE TRICK-OR-TREATERS!

Send us your innovative ideas for a way to scare them. In an effort to keep up with all of the new ways ghouls have developed for startling kids, we offer this reward. If you design or come across other effective pranks, tricks, yard layouts, haunted house scenes, or methods to make props, send them to us to share with others. If we use yours in an upcoming book, we will mention your name in the book and send you a free copy of our new booklet entitled "How to Carve Your Jack-o-lanterns in Just Seconds Using a Shotgun and a Chainsaw."

Send your ideas today: ☞ Chessmore Publishing Company
PO Box 16572
Chapel Hill, NC 27516 6572

Please fax any ideas to: ☞ HAUNTED CREATIONS
at: (919) 933-4789

Please e-mail any ideas to: ☞ boo@chessmorepublishing.com

So keep a sharp eye out around your home for new frightening ideas.

HOW TO SCARE TRICK-OR-TREATERS

This chapter may be the reason you bought this book. It's within these pages that we discuss all the devious ways you can repay those cute little trick-or-treaters who have been haunting you for years for a handout, then trashing your yard. This chapter has two sections, tricks to play on trick-or-treaters, and spooky layout scenes that can be set up in a garage, basement, on a porch, or in the front yard. The tricks can be a part of a layout scene, or used alone for Halloween fun. If one idea doesn't quite suit your needs, try to remodel it a little, it may become a perfect fit. We offer a lot of specific ideas, but also want to teach you to think up others by applying some of the basics we used in developing our tricks. The chapters "Haunted House Ideas" and "Halloween Party Fun" are laid out in the same format. We encourage you to read them as

well, even if your interests are only in scaring trick-or-treaters. But, before we get going, we feel obligated to discuss a few guidelines you might want to keep in mind while haunting the neighborhood:

1) Consider your audience and how it will vary in age and background. It can get embarrassing to have a four-year-old trick-or-treater breakdown into tears. It can be painful to have a 6'8" father show his appreciation for scaring three years of growth out of his 5-year-old pirate. Try to tone things down for those under 8, and never jump out and frighten a little one. Don't kid yourself, that trick-or-treater will keep growing, and someday they'll remember you.

2) Protect all exposed electrical wires, ropes, corners, overhangs, irregular walking surfaces and sharp edges from causing injury. Cover the aforementioned with tape and foam rubber, use reflective tape, or just eliminate the opportunity. Using radioactive props eliminates the need for lighting.

3) Don't frighten kids down steps. They lose orientation and their sense of balance when struck with a sudden surge of adrenaline. This causes an impulse reaction to evacuate the area immediately.

4) Be sure to have good liability coverage on your homeowner's insurance policy if you plan any tricks, or at least know a darn good lawyer.

5) Keep control of your haunted activities and any helpers used to scare the trick-or-treaters at all times. They should know their limitations, so if things get out of hand, be prepared to pull the plug before someone gets hurt.

6) Make sure that when props are rigged to jump out, fall, or swoosh by, that they do not come in direct contact with a visitor. Your casualty might be 6'4" weighing in at 240 lbs., and not have a good sense of humor, while everyone points to you saying, "He's did it!"

7) Don't eat candy found in your yard more than 5 days after Halloween.

TRICKS TO PLAY ON TRICK-OR-TREATERS

ALIVE OR A PROP:

In this trick we use a costume to disguise a helper to look like a prop. This may be a scarecrow or dummy costume with the character sitting limply in an awkward position on a porch, in a lawn chair, on a step, leaning up against a wall, or a tree, etc. As the unsuspecting trick-or-treater approaches, the character snaps to life. This works best when surrounded by several other dummies. Then, even if the kids have their suspicions, they still aren't sure which dummy is real. This can also be performed with a costume that looks like a pile of old rags, a bush, a pile of yard debris, a statue, yard decorations, or anything inanimate. Use painter's stilts for added height, and gloves on the ends of sticks for added arm length. To throw in a twist, use a headless dummy in a large chair with a helper hiding behind it covered with a black cloak, and his arms in the arms of the dummy.

THE LIVING DEAD:

Make 6-10 tombstones and have them positioned around the front yard. For added effect, include old sections of picket fence painted a weathered gray and white. Add an overhead sign "Bones-R-Us." Have one to three helpers costumed as corpses lie on the ground hidden and covered in leaves. When the trick-or-treaters ring the doorbell, the porch light flickers, then goes off. A loud sound effect of thunder comes on, while a camera strobe is flashed. Then a loud voice comes over the sound system

saying, "We've been waiting for you... for a long time." A strobe light illuminates the yard. The corpses come to life slowly out of their graves, each with a shovel, staggering toward the kids, while sound effects of Halloween moans and groans continue. If you don't mind messing up your front yard, dig a shallow open grave with dirt piled to the side, and a tombstone saying, "Room for one more!" Warn your helpers hiding in open graves to watch for stray dogs.

Note: This trick should be avoided in neighborhoods with a high percentage of mortician homeowners, all they'll do is to try to give out their business cards, or worse yet, steal your corpses.

EXPLODING HEAD:

This trick utilizes the dummy or scarecrow. For a different effect, make the head out of a large balloon, fill it with confetti, and use a black, wide-tipped marker to carefully draw a simple amateurish face. Gently mount the head on the shoulders of the dummy. Run bell wire with a model rocket engine igniter touching the back of the balloon at one end, and mount the other end to a remote hiding place with a 9 volt battery, where you can clearly see the kids (possibly indoors). Get the parts at a hobby shop. Also hide a speaker in or near the dummy, or run a dryer vent hose out to the dummy. The kids come up laughing at this ridiculous looking dummy, and a voice from the dummy says, "Boo! Did I scare you? Don't you think I'm scary?" When they yell, "No!" and laugh, the voice returns warning, "Then I'll show you!" Touch both ends of the wires to the battery, and boom! This can also be done using shaving cream, or filled with 2/3 water and 1/3 air in the balloon.

SURPRISE MAT:

This trick simply uses a mat switch device attached to a special effects device to surprise those little candy moochers. This could be a single flash (from a camera strobe) accompanied by a loud sound effect. Other effects can include:

- activating a small motor that pulls in the line attached to a hanging corpse on a track-line

- the use of a jackhammer pad that, when activated, vibrates like it's being jack hammered

- a ball of fire from a wired hidden flash device

- trigger a jump-out head on a spring board, or dropped from above on a black cord

The idea is a sudden surprise that doesn't harm anyone. You can use a loud horn or siren, rotating beacon lights, or turn on a compressor with a hose attached to a large balloon inside some hanging old clothes. The balloon explodes once it gets too large. Even small effects can be scary. Look around for other electrical special effects to trigger.

SPOOKY SHADOWS:

This display can also be performed from a front window as a silhouette on a white sheet or light colored opaque curtains or shades. One character can be sharpening an ax, or drinking a formula that turns him into a monster. Two characters can act out a struggle and murder. The wicked homeowner can use a prop of a trick-or-treater that he throws around. Use your imagination in developing a scary skit. You can also backlight these images with an old super 8mm movie, slide, video projector, or even cast shadows with other bright lights. Keep lights low outside. Consider using a strobe light for livelier shadowing.

SWOOPING BODIES:

This trick can be set up to approach trick-or-treaters either from the inside or the outside as they wait at the door. Use a figure, which could be a corpse, a dummy, a ghost, a skeleton, a witch, your mother-in-law, or anything else you have available. Attach it to a heavy duty fishing line, wire, or cable mounted at a sloped angle to allow for a rapid descent. One end of the line can be attached to a screw eye located above the front door, or to a point high enough above the kids' heads to prevent the figure from crashing into them, but coming close enough to scare them. The opposite end is your point of launch, and positioned high enough to provide a high speed and sloped descent.

When outside, this may be a tree, hill, basketball goal, garage roof peak, or anywhere you can have a hidden helper pull the figure into position, and release it upon demand. When performing indoors, the high end of the line can be mounted to the top of a flight of stairs, a high ceiling, or catapulted down a dark hallway. The figure has a black cord attached to it long enough to allow our dummy friend to be quickly pulled back into position for the next launch. The connection attaching the dummy bracket to the line can be a variety of hardware, like a small pulley, a metal hook, or anything that slides freely on the line. Keep the line taught for best speed. Combine this effect with a surprise strobe lighting, and a loud sound effect like a horn, a scream, or just a "Boo!"

LOST TRICK-OR-TREATER:

For added effect, have a plant (a helper dressed like another trick-or-treater) go up to the house with each group of other treaters. The ghost, monster, skeleton, corpse, vampire, witch, or whoever answers the door in costume grabs him at the front door, and drags him back into the house screaming and kicking (never to be seen again). A simpler approach is to have the plant trick-or-treater wear a fake arm that is attached with Velcro, so the monster at the door can rip it off (use only to scare older kids).

☠ Another figure to answer the door could include a headless man (headless torso prop available from reference vendors) or a floating head using luminous make-up.

☠ Finally, consider having a large corpse figure quietly slip in with the group from behind a parked car, a tree, or a large bush while they are heading for the door.

GIANT GHOST:

For a really big scare, make a 20' ghost puppet. Start with a very large balloon (18"-24" diameter). Make the head using the balloon covering it with several layers of newspaper strips and paper maché paste (mix 1.5 cups flour, 1 cup water, 1 tbs. Salt, and it's optional to add a couple of serious squirts of wood glue for strength.)

Once dry, position it under a very large section of light weight cloth (like cheese cloth) for the head shape, and carefully drill two small holes on the top about 3" apart. Attach a piece of fishing line to control the head.

Now for hands, get a pair of extra large black rubber gloves, and stuff them for shape. Hot glue the hands to the edge of the sheet with the palms facing outward, and tie heavy duty fishing line to each hand. These hands will be controlled like a marionette.

Using cheesecloth, sewing or hot gluing several sections around the base of the large cloth covering the head and hands until the desired length of the body is achieved. Each section will be the width of the fabric bolt used.

Attach three large 1" screw eyes to 3 locations across the top portion of the front of the house. Run the three lines into a second story window or operate from a safe spot on the roof. Let the ghost lie in a heap behind a bush, and as the kids approach, draw all three strings in to bring the ghost to life. Practice with line manipulations to improve your animated techniques. Use luminous or fluorescent paints under a UV light for added effect. Hot glue plastic tubing, chicken wire, metal weights, or something light weight around the inside base of the fabric to maintain shape under windy conditions. Use inexpensive fabric, since it will take up to about 12 yards.

You could also use plastic sheeting to save money. Connect pieces using duct tape or packing tape attached from the inside.

INFLATABLE SHOCKERS:

These little surprises can take a variety of forms, but the intention is to use a creature made out of inflatable material, have it lying inconspicuously near the front door, and at the right moment flip the switch to rapidly inflate the creature to life. The inflatable creature can be purchased as a Halloween decoration, or made out of an inflatable toy or decoration bought at a toy, novelty, gift, or Halloween store. It can also be made out of lightweight plastic trash bags, dry cleaner bags, disposable latex gloves (like those used by dentists), etc.

A simple and effective inflatable shocker is to make an arm. Start by cutting the sleeve off an old long-sleeve shirt. Get a lightweight, disposable latex glove, and a small waste paper can plastic liner cut to match the sleeve length. Cut the closed end of the bag off, lay the glove on a table, and insert about 1" of the bag inside the rubber glove, and use packing box tape to seal the glove to the bag. Use duct tape to securely fasten the other end of the bag around an air hose or a powerful hair dryer (set on cool). Either put a white lightweight cotton glove with blood stains over the rubber glove, or paint fake blood directly onto the rubber glove, then slide the shirtsleeve over the arm.

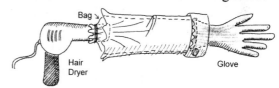

The lighter the materials, the faster the inflation. Take a hole punch and make 3-4 holes about 3" up from the end of the bag to keep it from popping from excessive inflation. Now, duct tape the dryer to the wall, or when using an air hose, tack the sleeve to the wall beside the door about 4' from the ground. Tape a section of black plastic sheeting onto the wall over the arm to keep it out of view. Then, only the extended arm will be visible to the treaters. From inside, wait for the kids to get close, and plug in the dryer (be sure to have the dryer switch preset to the on position).

The arm and hand will shoot straight out. Have other sound effects playing, so the noise made by the dryer isn't as distracting. Other figures that can be used include a large spider made with black plastic liners, or a ghost with white plastic liners. Make eyes, mouth and nose from pieces of paper, fabric, or cellophane. Use cellophane tape on seams, and cover in lightweight cloth for realism. The important thing is to keep it light enough to rapidly deploy, so test it out first. You can also use an air tank and compressor, but watch the pressure, or you may need to go over to the next block to recover your arm.

If you feel adventurous, install two arms, or you can even inflate a pair of hip boots.

SURPRISE BLOW UP:

Simply use an inflatable figure dressed in mask and overalls holding a lightweight chain saw made from cut and painted Styrofoam. A hidden operator rapidly inflates the figure using an attached air hose and tank at just the right moment. Be careful not to over inflate your little friend. This trick is also great using large inflatable creatures (without chain saws).

DROPPING IN:

This effect can be created by lowering overhanging figures from above, possibly a ghoul, dummy, or skeleton hanging by a noose. The figure may either be in plain view and lighted for the trick-or-treaters to see as they approach the house, or hidden in the shadows above. Don't actually hit anyone, but dropping it behind them is fine. Either do it quietly, so when they turn around they are greeted with a surprise, or drop the thing with great speed (attach cans and other noisy things to the dummy so it comes down with a loud crash). Then, raise it back up to life using unseen fishing lines like a puppet.

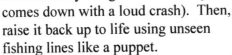

GROWING GHOST:

This effect can be made with a few pieces of 1" PVC pipe, a pair of old gloves, a Styrofoam wig stand, a spooky mask, and a large piece of opaque material sew into a hooded gown. Just lay flat on ground or hide behind house or bushes, then at the right time arise lifting your frame upward. You may need to cut a small flap to see through if you plan to walk around. You can also insert one piece of PVC into another with a fitting to extend.

UNWANTED HOST:

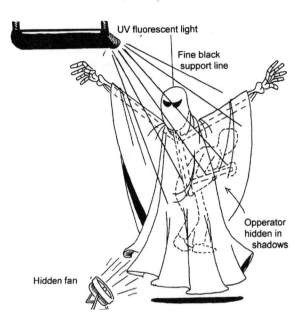

UV fluorescent light

Fine black support line

Opperator hidden in shadows

Hidden fan

In this trick the door is opened with a hidden line, and inside the door and down a hallway is what appears to be a free floating spirit. Our host can be either a character or a prop costumed as a ghost or skeleton. Use lightweight cheesecloth cut large enough to drape over character hanging about 3" above the floor to create the ghost. The person wears all black except white cloth gloves, and either a cheap mask painted black, a black hood, or black make-up. As the door opens (seemingly by itself because of black thread on knob), a fan, positioned on the floor to blow up into the ghost, causes the sheet to appear to be floating. A florescent UV light (black light) or multi-action strobe light is mounted above the door inside, out of view of the kids, and is shining down the hall, illuminating the figure. Use painter's stilts for added height. The background is shielded in black plastic sheeting. Be sure the costume glows well under the UV light. Also include spooky sound effects like screams, howls, or horns.

SURPRISE TREAT:

Cut a small piece if wood to the size of a candy bar. Notch out a section in the bottom about 2"x1" with it ¼"deep. Purchase a spring activated cap device and attach it into the notched hole in the bottom of the block. Wrap the top and four sides with a candy bar wrapper (be sure the cap device lies flat inside the notch). Leave the candy bar on a table beside a large bowl of other cheaper, smaller treats. Post a sign reading "please take just one, but leave candy bars for our friends." Hide and wait for a greedy trick-or-treater to pick up the bar. This can also be done with a pressure switch activating a loud horn and flashing lights.

Cap snapping device

Cap goes here

Fake Candy

You can also use a quick retracting device from a trick shop with a dollar bill attached lying on the front porch step. When they reach for it, poof, it's gone. In place of a candy bar, set the cap popper under a wallet with money sticking out.

Another effective trick is done with a latex baby puppet called "Baby Stinky". The puppet is wrapped in a baby blanket, and carried out the front door to show the trick or treaters the cute new baby. When the kids draw closer to see the infant, jerk the baby up at them from under the blanket with a loud growl or yell. The puppet is very ugly with a runny nose. Guaranteed to scare them every time. Look through the novelties sold on the web sites or catalogs of the vendors listed in the reference chapter for dozens of additional tricky ideas.

WINDY SURPRISE:

In this trick you'll need an air compressor with tank and about 75' of air hose. There are dozens of variations from this point on. You can rig the air hose by a mat and blow air up from below. You can also buy air mats that can spray air up from their feet. Another idea is to use the "Alive or a Prop" trick described earlier. Once the kids pass, (with your arms hidden inside the dummy out of sight) blow a loud air horn held in one hand, and shoot air through an air gun at the backs of their legs with the other. Be careful not to spray air in faces to avoid eye injuries. Afterward, allow time to collect all the candy the kids drop on their rapid departure.

BAD GHOST AT THE DOOR:

In this scenario, the host answers the door playing one of many simple practical jokes on unsuspecting trick-or-treaters. One is to have a "Plant" join the other kids at the door dressed as a ghost in a white sheet. The host greets the treaters, but is startled by the ghost, as if it were real, and shouts. "Watch out kids, I'll take care of that ghost!" Then the host begins hitting the planted ghost trick-or-treater with a stick, rubber ax, mallet, or a fly swatter, while blood rapidly appears to be coming from under the sheet. The trick is played with the host using a squeeze ball (from a drug store) filled with fake blood attached to plastic tubing (from a pet supply store) running down the sleeve to their wrist. As the host hits the ghost, he squeezes the ball, and blood squirts onto the white sheet. Another technique is for the ghost to have a water bottle with plastic hose filled with fake blood under the sheet. The ghost character screams, and runs around while being hit. Practice these techniques for realism. This scare is not recommended for younger kids. Obviously this may be one of several other pranks you could pull, otherwise in time, you'll run out of sheets. I'm sure that you can think of many variations of this (like the host acting like he's cutting his arm with a large knife trick).

Plastic tube

Fake
Blood

JACK-O-LAUGH-TERN:

Live Jack-O-Lantern
head on table

All you need here is to get an old card table, inexpensive round table, or 4'x4' sheet of 1' plywood and 4 prefabricated legs. Cut a hole into the top large enough to fit your head through. Buy a polyfoam jack-o-lantern, and cut the bottom out. Drape an old sheet or tablecloth over the table, cutting a hole in the tablecloth to match the hole in the table. Hide under the table, put your head through the hole, and have someone fit the jack-o-lantern over your head. Place a bowl of candy next to jack-o-lantern with a sign reading "Please, just take one." Come to life when some treater gets greedy.

Don't try this with a real pumpkin, unless you're the type that's not bothered when using outdoor portable toilet sheds.

This effect can also be done with a hand through a bowl of candy on a table. Try hiding a speaker inside or run dryer hose into the jack-o-lantern, and make it talk. Set off a camera strobe positioned inside the pumpkin using a remote flash switch cable sold at camera stores if someone tries to look inside.

This trick doesn't get you off the hook from carving a pumpkin. That's tradition brother, and it's unlucky to mess with tradition.

ON-COMING TRAFFIC:

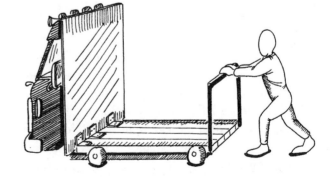

If you have a hallway connecting to the front entryway, leave all the interior lights off. When the doorbell rings, slowly open the door with a black thread, then flip on a bright spotlight shining right at the kids. Now, start the sound effect of a motor cycle starting up, then accelerating to a rapid speed. Jerk the light up slightly at this point, like the front end of a motor cycle would jump, then begin running toward the door with the light shining at the kids. Practice first for improved realism. There are many other variations to this trick, such as a train, a jet landing, or a space ship. Do whatever it takes to develop good sound effects, or buy prerecorded sound tapes or CDs. You can also make the front end of a bus, truck, or car. Attach it to a four wheel cart, and roll it at the front door for the same effect, only in this case use a faint flashlight, so the kids can see what's coming at them.

HIGH TECH DUMMY:

In this trick, take a small 9"-13" television, and mount it as the head on a dummy covering the back and sides with a hood, hat and collar, scarf, etc. to make it look like a head. Then connect a camcorder from a hidden location inside where you can see the trick-or-treaters. Put on a mask or make-up, sit in a chair or a stool in front of the camera where you can still see the kids. Be sure to drape black cloth behind your head as a background, and mount the camera on a tripod so it doesn't move. Zoom in on only your face, and try to keep your face in the camera field. When the kids come to the door won't they be surprised to meet a talking corpse that can see them.

Cable connects from behind, out of sight

Hidden TV set as head

Develop ways to scare these off-guard treaters. Try setting off a little lightning using a camera strobe with a loud thunder boom sound effect. Tease the trick-or-treaters about their costumes, or warn them that the house is haunted. There are hundreds of creative things to do with this skit. This trick is good for the little ones too, since it is not as scary.

BAT TO A VAMPIRE:

This trick requires a little additional help. Have someone stand to the side, out of view, inside the doorway about 12'-15' from the door. The only light will be a 24" UV fluorescent tube light ("Black Light"). The helper has a large rubber bat rigged to a fishing rod using non-fluorescent fishing line attached to both wings. Moving the end of the rod up and down will cause the wings to flap up and down as if floating in mid air.

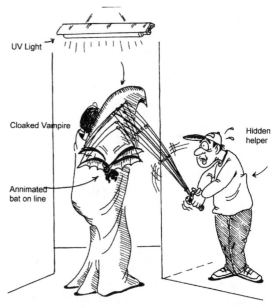

UV Light

Cloaked Vampire

Hidden helper

Annimated bat on line

Guest first see bat, then vampire appears

This can be rigged a variety of different other ways. One is to run each line through a separate screw eye attached to the ceiling or molding on opposite walls. The bat's features are highlighted in fluorescent paint to show up better under the UV light. The kids watch the bat for 3-5 seconds, just enough to know what it is. Then using either a pyrotechnic device from the Theater Effects company listed in the reference chapter, or a camera flash pointed out the front door out of view, give the kids a very bright flash. The bat is yanked out of view at the same second the vampire appears.

The vampire can be costumed in a large black cape, and already standing in the hallway behind the bat with its back turned and cloak draped over its head. To appear, the vampire spins around quickly, facing the UV light. Having the vampire use fluorescent make-up colors and a bright white or red vest will help it show up more brightly under the UV light. This illusion can also be done changing a large spider into a witch, a floating skull into a skeleton, etc. Practice with positioning, movement, lighting, and costume colors to get a truly professional look.

PIZZA DELIVERY MAN:

While the kids are walking up to the door, a pizza deliveryman pulls quickly into the driveway, hopping out, and hurrying up to the door with a pizza box in hand. As he joins the kids waiting for the occupant to open the door, he removes his mask or make-up that made him look like an ordinary person, and underneath is the face of a hideous corpse. The pizza man now drops the pizza box, and begins going after the trick-or-treaters shouting, "I love the taste of the little ones" in a horse deep voice.

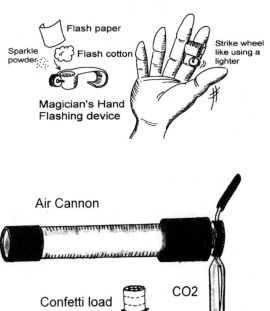

The challenge here is to get the phony face to look real and the make-up or mask underneath it to look like a ghoul. Wear gloves over fake monster hands for even greater effect. Remove the gloves after dropping the pizza boxes. Sorry, no coupons accepted by this guy. This effect works best with a surplus pizza delivery uniform available at many thrift stores. You can also use a latex pizza covered with body parts from a Halloween shop.

PYROTECHNIC SURPRISE:

In the reference chapter is a company that lists a wide variety of pyrotechnic special effect props. One is a magician's hand flasher. This device can discharge a bright flash, ball of fire, or shower of sparks suddenly from your hand. This effect is great when greeting the kids at the door, (no porch lights on) and warning them that this treat candy is very hot, then FLASH! They'll jump every time. They also sell CO2 confetti cannons that make sound and blow air and confetti.

Learn how to operate these items safely before attempting to use them around others.

Flash paper

Sparkle powder

Flash cotton

Strike wheel like using a lighter

Magician's Hand Flashing device

Air Cannon

Confetti load

CO2

MYSTERY FOG:

You can produce fog with either a tub of dry ice in warm water, or a fog machine. Fog machines are available for rent, but you have to reserve one months in advance. You could try to borrow one from a university theatrical department. Fog machines are expensive to buy, costing from $200 up to $5,000. There is also a product that is smoke effect in an aerosol can that lasts up to 5 minutes which sells for $15-$20.

In the fog, who knows what might come out of the bushes. Also, play with strobe or UV lighting for added effect, but be careful not to disorient little ghosts and witches right off the porch steps. From an open window, use a squirt gun through the fog on the unsuspecting treaters. You can also use canned spray string.

SELF-INFLICTED PAIN:

In these illusions, a crazed scientist or prisoner uses old magician tricks to look as though he is either sticking needles through his body, cutting off a limb, or just making slices. These illusions are fairly simple to perform.

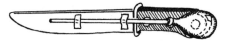

The knife slicing the skin requires a rubber squeeze bulb (used for babies and to remove water from ears) filled with fake blood, and attached to a section of plastic tubing that feeds the fake blood to the blade. The bulb is hidden in the user's hand, and squeezed to make blood look like it's coming from the cut.

Before performance rubber cement a fold of forearm skin together, then slide the long pin through this fold

The long needles are held between folded skin that is stuck together with rubber cement or spirit gum. The needle looks like it is going through the skin.

1-2-3 SURPRISES:

Here we simply hide in the bushes with our compressor, camera flash, and loud siren whistle and at the appropriate moment shoot air through the bushes at the trick-or-treater's legs, while flashing the strobe on the camera and blowing the siren whistle. Quite effective, and fun!

FISHING FUN:

You can do a lot more than fish with a fishing rod and reel around Halloween. Find yourself a comfortable chair, and pull it up to a second story window facing the front of the house. With room lights off and door closed, get ready to have some real fun haunting the trick-or-treaters. Attach a medium sized rubber bat to the line, and sail it over the kid's heads, or drag a rat or snake across the yard. Dangle a large rubber spider on someone's head. Attach the line to a low tree or bush limb, and make it jump up at passing kids. Make a lightweight ghost come whizzing across the yard at lightning speed. Illuminate the object internally with a small flashlight, or use luminous paint.

You may need a little practice in advance. However, once you get good, you could set up small witches, skeletons, spiders, or even a life-size cut out of their old math teacher. With experience, you can lower a big wad of chewed gum into a trick-or-treater's bag, and get a treat of your own. Even try lowering a camera strobe flash on a timer.

DECIDE YOUR CHOICE MIX OF SURPRISES:

With a little imagination, there are enough untapped ideas that we could fill another book. Don't let your fear to be different "hang you" up when haunting. Whatever you decide, have fun, and remember, it never hurts to keep in shape practicing your high speed sprinting. Also learn a foreign language.

HAUNTING SCENE IDEAS FOR TRICK-OR-TREATERS

Now we get to your first real challenge of the book. Your Halloween scene will be a composite of bits and pieces gathered from throughout this book, as well as from the depths of your imagination.

This section of the chapter will include examples to give you ideas on how to position and group your props, characters, effects, and tricks to produce the best impact. Each concept illustrates a scene you can use as a whole, or take the pieces to create you own. The secret is in the art of molding these pieces to fit into your own unique scene. Your budget, space, time to prepare, theme, talent, and the desired effect on those lovely little trick-or-treaters are also factors.

Add dimension to a normally boring Halloween porch scene with the addition of a large costumed butler resembling Lerch from the Addam's Family.

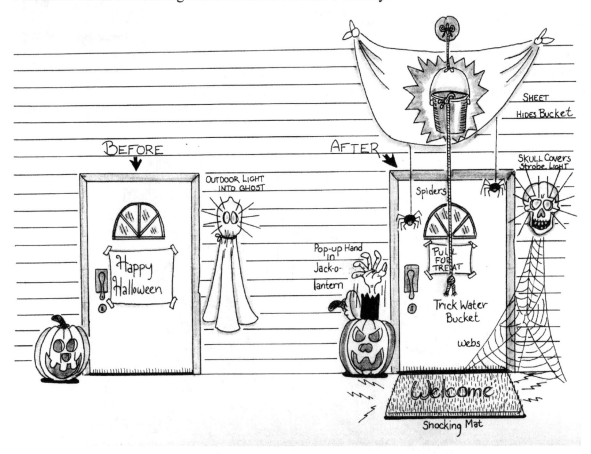

Oh yes, when you see the term "character" used it means some human volunteer crazy enough to dress up as part of the scene. As an incentive, offer them all the candy the trick-or-treaters drop as they run off in sheer terror. When more props are used, fewer characters are needed.

GRAVEYARD: YARD SCENE

- A variety of tombstones populate the yard, comical epitaphs can be used (see Chapter 5).

- Use corpse props around as though they are coming up out of the graves. Use leaves, yard clippings, black plastic bags, or something that resembles disturbed dirt, (but will clean up easily) around the props to add to the effect (horse or cow droppings, not a good idea).

- Use a coffin (see Chapter 5 - Props) as the centerpiece, have a costumed corpse, skeleton, ghost, or vampire character inside to pop out, and hand out the candy. (I'm reminded of an old expression Mom always told us boys, "Don't forget to close the lid when you're through." Any ghoul worth his weight in maggots need not be reminded to close the coffin lid for the next group of kids).

- Use spooky sound effects from a hidden boom box using a Halloween tape or CD.

- Light the area with strobe or yard-level spotlights (protect cords against tripping-'treaters).

- If you have a tree, hang ghosts or a dummy (see Chapter 5 - Props), or use the pulley system trick described earlier in the Giant Ghost. This scene can be a lot of fun…on the bigger kids.

- Use pieces of an old picket fence from an abandoned house if available, make and weather an old sign saying "caution, body crossing."

- Have costumed characters also covered in leaves coming up out of their graves.

- Hang black ground cover fabric as a backdrop to a grave.

25

CARNIVAL FORTUNETELLER: GOOD SCENE FOR THE PORCH

- The centerpiece is a small table covered with an old mystic colored tablecloth.

- The character sits at the table dressed as the old fortune teller (or use an attractive fortuneteller, appropriately costumed, if you want to lure the dads over too).

- The crystal ball can be a variety of things (see Chapter 5 - Props) in this case we'll suggest 4"-5" light fixture globe.

- Use a small light inside crystal ball with a foot pedal switch for effect.

- If you can cut holes in the table you're using, have a small black bottomless box with a hinged top that a "thing" hand can pop out of to hand out candy. Have the fortuneteller ask trick -or-treaters to place their hand on her crystal ball for her to tell their fortune (this will be the signal given to "Thing" character under the table to pop their hand out).

- Hang unusual mysterious props around for effect (tambourines, rubber chickens, etc).

- Use hanging lamp or shop light with low watt or orange bulb and make and decorate a round half-globe lampshade to cover bulb.

FUNERAL: A PORCH OR YARD SCENE,

- The centerpiece will be a coffin on a cloth covered table sturdy enough to support the weight of the coffin and corpse character inside.

- Attendees for the deceased can be either dummies or characters (of course properly dressed for the occasion) seated around in chairs.

- Pallbearers may be floating ghosts (supported by a chicken wire frame hidden under their sheets) grasping the handles.

- The usher character leads trick-or-treaters up to coffin to pay their respects. Character inside coffin throws coffin lid open to pass out treats (if anyone is left to give treats to).

- Keep lighting low. Have a low watt or orange bulb over the coffin at a minimum. Turn on strobe and turn other lights out when coffin opens for effect (be advised that if there are steps, a sudden shock may not be a good idea, since children often miss steps when adrenaline levels peak from blinding fright).

- Have funeral organ music playing from a hidden boom box (usually found on many Halloween tapes or CDs).

- The background may include using black plastic, cardboard, or a dark sheet as a backdrop. As props, use candle sticks, old songbooks, or anything else you might find in an old funeral parlor (visit one for ideas, just don't take anything, the walls have eyes!).

ALIEN SPACESHIP ACCIDENT: A YARD SCENE

- ☠ The centerpiece will be a spaceship that can be made from a kid's swimming pool, scrap wood and cloth, trash cans, etc. (get creative, borrow your neighbor's meat smoker).

- ☠ Lighting is very important here, use flash beacons, strobes, or other colored flashing lights that would resemble landing or emergency lights (you want it to be confusing and disorienting).

- ☠ Have characters dressed like aliens lying very still on the ground near the crash site. When the kids approach for their treats, both aliens jump to life shooting the kids with space gun (prop can be a toy space gun that makes noise, lights up, or made from spray string in a can, just use something that will create a surprise noise, lights, or effects).

- ☠ Have loud eerie sounds playing from hidden boom box as the kids approach, then just as aliens jump to life, change to very loud warning horns or sirens and turn on strobe.

- ☠ Use dry ice in a tub of warm water or fog machine positioned under spaceship for added effect (you can rent fog machines or save money and burn dozens of large cheap cigars).

- ☠ Scatter odd props around the crash site such as scrap pieces of heating duct, large unusual parts, bread makers, or anything that looks like it could have fallen from a space ship.

- ☠ Have a large cardboard box marked "specimens" in large modern font lettering, inside the box use something that can make noise, like these battery operated balls that roll by themselves, to add to the effect (you can get gross and use rubber body parts in the box).

MAD SCIENTIST LAB: A GARAGE OR PORCH SCENE

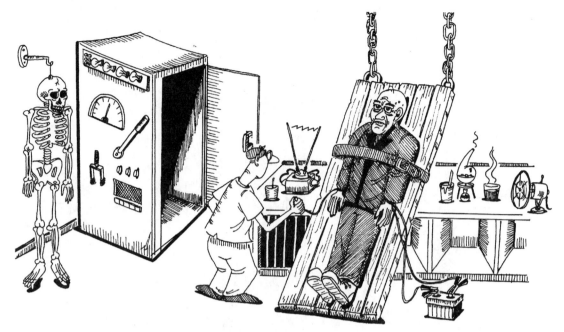

☠ The centerpiece is a large upright board or table with a large lifeless monster securely shackled or strapped in place with large jumper cables connecting to the monster

☠ A large appliance box is painted black with buttons, lights, and a large fork switch is positioned near the table as a prop to add atmosphere if needed

☠ Other props can include a table filled with typical laboratory equipment, beakers, test tubes, dry ice in clear bowls or containers of colored water

☠ Also, include small motor spinning a hypnotic cardboard circle wheel, include skeletons, skulls, body parts, etc.

☠ Use as many low watt colored flashing lights as possible with one center light (green or orange) that is on the monster (spot or overhanging)

☠ Use two boom boxes, one constantly playing eerie background sounds of bubbling, electric sparks snapping, weird sounds etc., the other boom box will be used for loud sound effects that are switched on when lever is thrown

☠ The evil scientist in a blood-spattered coat greets the trick-or-treaters shouting, "My little friend is about to come to life, come watch." When the large lever is flipped, all other lighting goes out. A strobe is focused on the monster along with the loud sound effects come on for about ten seconds with volume constantly increasing until monster jumps to life. Snapping the straps or shackles, he jumps out at the scientist, choking him, then turning to the kids saying in a sweet voice "time for your treats," only to hand out candy.

☠ With hands in black socks hidden through holes under shackles, use prop hands shackled for the kids to see. The scientist begins to whip or torture the monster until he can't take it anymore, and breaks free of the shackles leaving the prop hands still shackled (looks like hands gone which are inside black socks). The monster then chases the kids before the executioner gives out treats.

TORTURE CHAMBERS: A GARAGE OR PORCH SCENE

- ☠ Create a backdrop on either cardboard or a sheet painted to look like stone wall, you can also buy plastic sheeting backgrounds at a party supply store or use dark drop cloth.

- ☠ Shackle prop skeletons to wall. Hang bats (the flying kind, not the baseball kind,) large spiders, and rat props around for effect.

- ☠ Create rack torture table (see Chapter 5 - Props). Have tortured costumed character exposed in the upper half of the table, wide waste tie down (either fake leather belt, ropes, sheeting, etc.) separating upper and lower halves of the racked character's body.

- ☠ Masked disfigured torturer/executioner character steps out and begins turning rack wheel laughing with character howling, then acts like the wheel can't go further, giving it one more tug, lower body snaps off, upper body left howling and flailing, executioner says, "oops!" and comes after kids with double-bladed ax.

- ☠ Another approach is to have a character to be executed lay head down on chopping block or mock guillotine with prop head, and executioner chops off head, then headless body (character costumed w/o head) arises, chasing the kids before giving out treats.

- ☠ Play a Halloween tape of moaning, groaning, and screams on hidden boom box.

MONSTER MARKET: YARD SCENE

☠ Several small tables can be set up like a market place, have a few neighbors join in, each with their own table of "treats" to hand out… like a block-treat party.

☠ Each table is set up with the characters costumed as various types of ugly monsters selling hideous merchandise. One may have cooked spaghetti as brains with the trick-or-treaters required to pick their wrapped treat out of the wet spaghetti.

☠ One booth has body parts for sale with a monster offering wrapped bubble gum eyeballs as treats.

☠ One booth may be selling human heads asking trick-or-treaters if they would be willing to sell theirs, or maybe trade for a larger model.

☠ One booth might be selling evil magic potions in jars and bottles. Make labels using your imagination. You could have an inexpensive light-weight costume or outfit (like pajamas) starched, hanging in the back of the booth with a very fine fishing line to appear to be floating, the kids can be told that this little trick-or-treater tried out the invisibility potion.

☠ Another booth might be selling spiders, bats, rats, bugs, snakes etc. If you can buy candy bugs or snakes, the shop vender can eat one in front of the kids.

☠ One booth might be selling weapons or instruments of torture (for the older kids).

☠ Each booth vendor tries to attract kids to their booth for a treat, like the "Barkers" at a carnival.

☠ Lighting can be overhead low watt hanging lights in each booth (shop lights).

EVIL MAGICIAN'S STAGE: GARAGE, BASEMENT, OR PORCH SCENE

FOR AN OLDER GROUP OF TRICK-OR-TREATERS:

- The centerpiece is a mock stage. Use a table covered in fancy but aged tablecloth reaching the floor.

- On the table, position a magician's magic saw box with the character laying down with her actual head and arms sticking out of the top half of the box, and prop legs and feet sticking out of the bottom. Attached the legs to a control rod so the character can operate them.

- The character locked in the box beckons for the trick-or-treaters to come release her before the mad evil magician, "Dr. Psyconuts" (get creative with the name), returns to saw her in half.

- Hang an old sheet as a half drawn curtain, and the mad magician character jumps out with a live chain saw (without chain), and starts cutting box in half with character inside the box screaming.

- Other props could include rubber skulls and skeletons or other spooky things a magician might use (rubber chicken, a rabbit with elephant ears, top hat with eyes, floating gloves).

- Use overhead spotlights to illuminate stage, and have low volume background instrumental music, like stage performers use, playing from a hidden boom box.

- Toss treats from the stage to any brave kids remaining.

- If you want to get nasty, get a large old umbrella, fill a large balloon with shaving cream and air, and attach it to the outside tip of the umbrella. With umbrella open, the magician claims the balloon will magically pass through the umbrella upon his mystic command. The umbrella is aimed at the trick-or-treaters, the magic words are shouted while a large pin is extended through the umbrella from the inside by the magician, popping the balloon, sending cream onto the kids.... How could you?

HAUNTED CARNIVAL:

- A variety of small booths are set up using small covered tables, old chairs, and a variety of other spooky carnival theme oriented props.

- Each booth is some eerie dark carnival sideshow. An old sheet can be propped up to resemble an old carnival canvas tent. Use either costumed dummies or volunteer characters to occupy each tent.

- Hang trapeze bars from a tree limb or porch ceiling (swing set chain and bars made with wood dowel rod and screw eyes) with corpse, skeleton, or ghost figures hanging from them. Create a swinging movement.

- One sideshow may be an old fortuneteller, seated at a dark cloth covered table with crystal ball and tarot cards on top as props (see Chapter 7 Props for crystal ball ideas).

- Another booth may be for the one-eyed knife thrower whose aim isn't what it use to be. This can be evidenced by the skeleton volunteer costumed with wig as a once lovely assistant standing against the wall surrounded by miss-thrown knives struck into the wall, chest, arms, etc. Draw up comical carnival promotion posters.

- Another booth can be some kind of sideshow freak, such as the fat person, the two headed man, four armed lady, eight legged spider person, etc. Make a dummy or use costumed character. Some people may take offense to mocking the physically challenged. If this happens, ask if they would mind manning the sideshow booth instead of the freak. If they accept, you can entitle the booth "Oversensitive Left-winged Liberal."

- If you want to have some fun, devise the caged woman that turns into a gorilla trick (See Chapter 2 Tricks to Play).

- One booth may have a strange animal that can be made up as a prop. You can have fun with this one. Try the three legged dog surrounded by fire hydrants or an animal with a human head using a character inside the animal costume with his human head sticking out (remember your theme: humor, horror, whatever…).

- If you have an old mannequin or …blow-up doll, you can cover it with kids transfer tattoos calling it the tattooed lady, use your imagination for other booths

- Other props may include haunted junk food booths, ticket booths manned by ghosts or skeletons, ring the bell with a mallet (with a prop human head on the end of the mallet), instead of duck pond use rubber bats, spiders, rats, skulls, mini jack-o-lanterns or any other idea you may dream up

- Make cages out of a painted frame using 2"x4" s and 1"x 3/8" trim board for bars. Make a large spider with legs out of black painted dryer vent hose or yard drainage pipe, body out of a stuffed heavy-duty black plastic garbage bag.

For fun set on table with a hole to allow a human head to be the head of the spider

Your creativity will provide the key to come up with dozens of others. Remember to try to use what you already have, can make, or can afford to buy. Try to get some idea of how much time to allow for set up, so you're ready in time. Plan to finish your set up by about one hour before sunset (check your local paper) on Halloween, and take the scene down that night, after the last of the trick-or-treaters float off into the darkness, to maintain the mysterious nature of your layout. It takes a fraction of the set-up time for tear-down.

If you are planning an elaborate layout, think about contacting your local newspaper to see if they might want to take a photo for the morning edition. Of course, if you go all out and make a haunted garage, basement, attic, or house you may want to be open for several days.

Oh yes, remember to tell those attorneys that you just lost your job when they come back with their kid screaming, "lawsuit." You can't blame us, we wrote this as a humor book. We never expected anyone to be crazy enough to actually try any of this stuff!

Please read on through the Haunted House and Party chapters for other ideas that could also be used on trick-or-treaters. Also join the "Halloween-l" e-mail list for haunters of all kinds by submitting an e-mail to listserv@netcom.com with "subscribe halloween-l youremail@address" typed in the body of the post (nothing else). Be prepared to get between 25 to 150 e-mails a day depending on the time of year, but great stuff. If you open a free email site these list e-mail can be kept separate.

HAUNTED HOUSE IDEAS

This chapter is dedicated to both the curious and to anyone ambitious enough to develop a haunted attraction at their home or a school. As with the chapters for trick-or-treaters and the chapter on parties, this chapter is divided into two sections. The first section describes various illusions used in haunted attractions. The second section discusses a variety of layout scene ideas.

We realize that most of the tricks in this section are more advanced than the average person will attempt. However, we hope that as you learn the techniques behind these tricks, you call upon your imagination, and design a simpler version that better fits your resources. Consider what kinds of things frighten people? Maybe a piece of large machinery that could be designed to look like it was about to crush the patrons. Possibly a large bird swooping down, hands crawling by themselves, large insects creeping down a wall, a person on a rotisserie stake over an oven, an old woman in a wheelchair elevator flying down a flight of stairs at you, or many others. The secret is to learn to use your creativity from two perspectives. What scares people or catches them by surprise, and how can that sensation be built into an illusion? It certainly gets easier with experience, but the greatest reward is the benefit you'll reap by learning how to routinely use your creativity in finding solutions to new challenges.

This chapter should give you plenty of ideas to get started. The tricks and illusions require far less preparation than do complete layout scenes, so if you just want to have a little fun, skip the scenes, and just set your favorite tricks. As you gain experience in constructing these tricks, learn more about the special effects, and discover the tricks available for purchase, you'll be designing hybrid tricks of your own. It's like working a crossword puzzle, you start to develop a talent for it.

HAUNTED HOUSE ILLUSIONS

In this section we describe tricks often used in haunted houses. The more money invested, the more sophisticated the tricks become. We encourage you to spend some time browsing vendor web sites to see how elaborate these illusions and special effects can get. If you're on a limited budget, you'll be amazed at what a little imagination can do to develop tricks from inexpensive materials. Any resemblance between our readers and characters pictured in this book is purely coincidental. We included that disclaimer because you never know when you're going to be sued by a "Toon."

THE MAZE:

The maze is best suited for situations where there is an abundance of space. We provide a sample floor plan, but refer to a children's maze puzzle book to find other simple wall patterns. Tricks that can be played on those attempting to pass through the maze include:

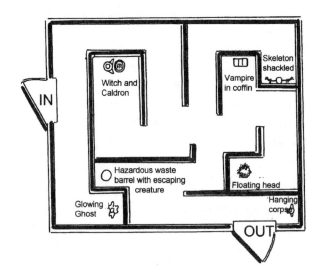

- ☠ Characters costumed in dark robes with ugly make-up, vampires, werewolves, etc. lurking in corners (avoid latex masks since visibility is limited and they get hot to wear for extended periods). The actors can approach the guests, but should try to avoid physical contact to prevent injury.

- ☠ Strobe lighting adds to the tension and confusion.

- ☠ Keep the wall patterns the same. Many people just use black plastic sheeting.

- ☠ Have maniacal laughter playing as background sound.

- ☠ Use a fog machine to increase the challenge of passage.

- ☠ Have emergency lighting and signage in case of emergency.

- ☠ Build walls securely enough to withstand the crowds' prodding.

SURPRISE TRUNK - SPRING-BOARD HEAD:

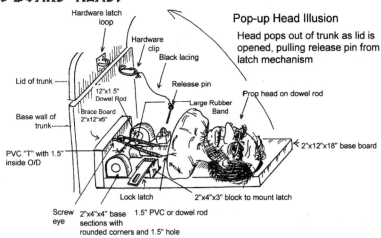

This trick utilizes a prop head that triggers to life upon opening the trunk. The trick requires you to have an old trunk (found at garage sales, flea markets, import shops, second-hand stores, or attics). You'll also need a nasty looking head prop. The most effective choice would be to use a corpse or skeleton head prop that also has the shoulder attached. You can also use a plastic skull model or Styrofoam wig stand with a mask.

To build the device pictured you'll need a 12" section of 1" or larger dowel rod and a section of 1.5" PVC pipe 14" long (or enough to stand the head completely out of the trunk once the lid is opened). You'll also need an 18" section of 2"x12" board, one 6" section of 2"x12" board, (2) sections of 2" x 4" x 4" board, (2) 2" x 4" x 3" sections of board, a latch clasp used with a pad lock, a 1.5" PVC "T" fitting, and a wide rubber band about 5"-6" long. The PVC pipe connects the head to the "T" fitting. The dowel rod is used to hinge the PVC pipe to the base supported by side bracket blocks. The end brace board connects the rubber band to the PVC pipe to act like a spring. See diagram for construction details. The head is latched down in the spring set position, with the unit resting on the floor inside the trunk. The lock pin is inserted and the other end clipped to the inside of the lid. This can only be set when the lid is almost closed, since the string is just long enough to reach so the pin is released when the lid is fully opened. Pulling out the pin pops the latch open (from upward force of PVC pipe), and the head pops out of the trunk.

This device can also be mounted to a wall or door with a window.

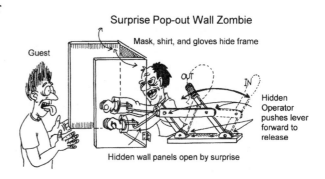

Surprise Pop-out Wall Zombie

Mask, shirt, and gloves hide frame

Guest

OUT   IN

Hidden Operator pushes lever forward to release

Hidden wall panels open by surprise

A similar effect can be achieved by building a dummy that swings open window shutters and pops out at guests as they pass in a hallway. The dummy has fake hands and arms attached to the inside door handles, a stuffed torso, and a wig stand with full head mask or fake severed head. The mechanism is operated from behind the figure by a helper.

MYSTERIOUS TRANSFORMATION CHAMBER:

This is an illusion used for many years in carnivals and State Fair midway shows. The concept is to transform one figure into another figure right before your eyes. The illusion can be used with a variety of subjects; vampire to a bat, man to a corpse or skeleton, attractive woman to a witch or animal. The technique is simple, but these ground rules must be followed to establish a realistic illusion:

Original Subject

Transformed Subject

Lights

Glass or Mirror

Audience

- ☠ The two rooms (see drawing) must be decorated identically, so the fewer the props and simpler the wall no patterns, the easier it is to reproduce.

- ☠ The rooms must be square and of the same dimensions. They should have walls no less than 4' and no longer than 12' for best effect.

- ☠ The figures should be positioned identically in each room.

- ☠ Lighting is controlled by rheostat or dimmer switches and adjusted to diminish in the room with the first figure at the same pace, and level as the light in the second room is increased, creating a morphing illusion. Perform this fairly quickly, so as not to give things away.

☠ When using regular glass plate, use lower watt lighting (40-60), when using 2-way mirrored glass or screened glass use a brighter light (100-150 watt) in the room the first subject is in. Also, have the mirrored side of the glass facing the audience.

☠ Practice until the desired effect is achieved.

☠ The room lighting is above the front of the room, facing into the room, and shining onto the figures. This gives the best effect.

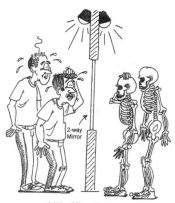

2-Way Mirror Illusion

A similar illusion can also be performed in a simpler arrangement by using a two way mirror with the audience looking at their reflection or an image screened onto the glass, and then have the lighting come up on the other side to show a ghoul, monster, skeleton, etc. Use a wall mirror, framed picture, or full-length mirror. Make sure the light level on the backside is not too bright. You want the audience to still see their own reflection. This illusion makes it look like someone or something is behind them. The room on the opposite side of the glass should be fairly narrow, and draped in black (plastic sheeting or fabric or painted). The morphing effect can be used for small wall mirrors with costumed helpers on the opposite side that can mimic the on-looking guest as the lights from behind come up.

ENDLESS HALLWAY:

As you can see in the drawing, this hallway is a good addition to any maze, or great to just occupy a hallway between rooms. Mirrors positioned at a 45 angle will not reflect the person's image in the hallway, ceiling and walls are black with white stripes, and the floor is some dark color.

Floor is a
dark color

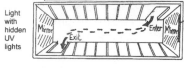

Light
with
hidden
UV
lights

CAMOUFLAGE ROOM:

Decorating all four walls of a room in a single pattern, like white dots on black, small stripes or any design creates this illusion. The room is lit with flashing strobe lights, and there are loud background sounds playing (screaming, moans, etc). Then position a character dressed entirely in the wall pattern against a wall. As the patrons pass through the room the character sneaks up on them with short quick moves to match the strobe rate. This can also be done with a jungle or forest scene. The trick is to match costume with background pattern, and movements with strobe light speed.

BODY PARTS ILLUSION:

This trick has been discussed throughout the book in differing variations, but it uses the same props and techniques. You need to get a 4'x8' by 1" or thicker sheet of plywood and two saw horses, or an old table that you no longer need that is at least 72" long and 40" wide. The trick is just as you would imagine. Cut holes into the top of the table or boards to allow the character to fit whichever real parts are to be exposed or hidden (depending on whether the person lies on top of the table or underneath the table - lying on a hidden shelf). This is usually the head and possibly one or all of the limbs. If you only wish to expose a head or hand, use a smaller table. In either case, use a white cloth with bloodstains. Cut holes in the cloth which correspond to those in the table. The moving of the live parts and the moans to add to the effect.

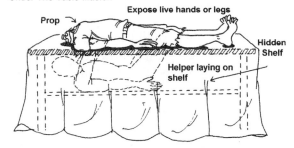

Under The Table Illusion

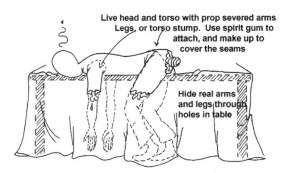

On Top of Table Illusion

PENDULUM TORTURE TABLE:

In this trick the head, arms, and legs stick up out of the holes with the character's bottom resting on the hidden shelf. Use the same type illusion props as above with the torso of the body as the prop to be cut. For safety, fabricate the blade be from painted cardboard or Styrofoam. Use 1" PVC pipe conduit for the pole swinging the blade. The swinging hinge can be fabricated in a variety of ways. Glue a tight-fitting end-cap with a screw eye in the middle into the ceiling end of the PVC pipe. The ceiling assembly should have two braces with holes for a pin to slide through both side brackets and the screw eye in the end cap. The swinging action can be either motorized or maintained by a helper.

Strobe lights add an eerie effect. Also, place around the scene, plenty of skulls, bones, rats, and large spiders with webs. Make the backdrop look like gray stone block. Lighting with a lamp oil yard torch also adds to the crude atmosphere.

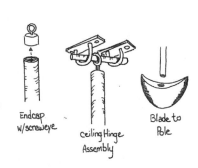

PHONY PORTRAIT:

Get an old portrait painting, or have an art student paint up a quickie. Buy a set of fake eyes (see Chapter 7). Make a pivoting device and attach it to a motor (like the type used in inexpensive motorized animated Christmas decorations). Then, cut out the portrait eyes and mount this device behind the painting so the eyes seem to slowly shift back and fourth. You can position fixed eyes as pictured.

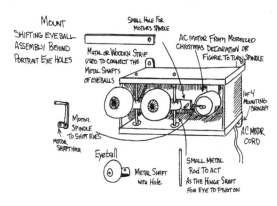

An additional approach is to have the portrait silk screened onto a lightweight fabric or glass, and then illuminate a hideous face from behind the portrait. Alternatively, project a changing image onto a blank picture frame.

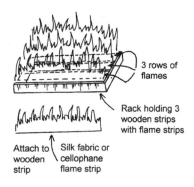

ILLUSION OF FIRE:

This illusion uses an air-blowing device like a small fan, or hair dryer, irregularly cut strips of red, orange, and yellow satin fabric, foil, or cellophane, and red, blue, and orange lighting.

Cut irregular flame strips that can be hot-melt glued to cross-sections of wood cut from 1"x 1/4" stock. These wood sections are then built into a frame consisting of 3-6 rows to give a three dimensional effect to the flames. Depending on where you want the fire to come from, the rack is mounted in such a way to allow a small fan or hair dryers positioned to be blowing from underneath to create the flapping movement of the lighted fabric strips resembling flames. The colored lights add to the realism. Practice positioning the lights and fan until the desired effect is achieved. This illusion looks best from a distance of at least 20'. Even when designing a single one row of fabric configuration, the effect can still be somewhat realistic. Use burning sound effects to drowned-out the noise of the fan. Cut the flame strips with much longer flames for a varied 3D look.

CREATURE WITH HUMAN HEAD OR FLOATING HEAD:

Perform this effect with a mirror to hide the lower body of the character. Make a prop table or chair with the mirror positioned at a 45 angle to reflect the floor or chair seat surface. Place the body behind it. The background behind the head must match that of the floor or seat pattern reflected by the mirror. Attach the prop of the creature's body (a bat or spider) to a board that is positioned at a 45 angle above the head. Position a mirror at a 45 angle below the head to reflect a floor pattern that must match the backdrop.
For support, and to add effect, build the scene is in a small cage.

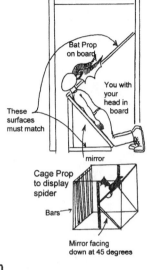

Use the same trick is used to float a head. These can be great illusions when properly designed and lighted.

Table

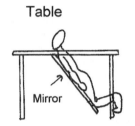

Mirror

Chair

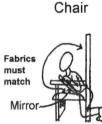

Fabrics must match

Mirror

CRAZY ROOM EFFECTS:

In this trick the tilted floor requires a sub floor and ceiling that are booth positioned parallel to each other. This is best suited for areas with limited square footage of floor space, like a hallway. Keep the angle no more than 20 degrees, and be sure to paper and decorate the walls in a 90 angle to the floor to create the illusion. With the furniture on the wall or ceiling, the illusion is to make the

patrons walk through the room passing around ceiling fans, lights, pictures, doors, etc. The more detail props you can add like nick-knacks on table tops, clocks, paintings, etc., the better the effect. There are illusion designs to make people of the same size look very different. This is done by creating unusual floor and wall angles, use a browser key word search on "illusion".

You may want to add another dimension by making a chair rock by itself. Secure the chair to the ceiling with a hinge assembly similar to the one described for the pendulum attached at the center of each of the chair's rocker blades. Use a small motor and some light test fishing line to make a chair rock by itself.

Get a clock, remove the works, and with an electric motor run the shaft into the face of the clock, attach the hands, and operate the motor to rotate the hands counterclockwise at a much faster speed than clocks normally run. Get the motor from a small electronics shop like Radio Shack[®].

Another effect is to create a falling room or elevator by positioning brick or wall surfaces on a roller device by the windows of the room or elevator, using small motors, or a crank to spin the rolls at high speed. If making an elevator, position it on rollers or large springs in the corners to create movement effects.

Also make fake walls on wheels to roll in as if the walls will crush guests, flicker lighting or strobe lights for additional effect.

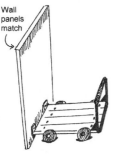

Wall panels match

Roll wall panels on carts in toward guest, using multiple panel carts

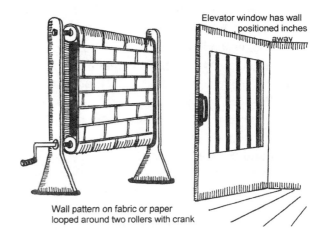

Elevator window has wall positioned inches away

Wall pattern on fabric or paper looped around two rollers with crank

HIGH-TECH SURVEILLANCE:

The effect here is to have a ghoulish ghost greet your guests via what appears to be videotape. However, the host mysteriously has the ability to interact with his guests.

Place a TV (13"-19") in a haunted room. Have it connected to a long camcorder cable in another room. Make sure the person who will be on the TV can see the guests in the room. Behind the character being taped use a backdrop or set to be that accommodates the situation. Script what you want your costumed actor to say. For a spaceship, layout this may involve the warning of an escaped space specimen. In a haunted house it may be the visiting spirit of the house's prior owners.

The better the drama of the script, the more effective reaction you get from the audience. Use other high-tech props like St. Elmo's fire (use caution when using electricity). Or, fill a small, round, lighted aquarium with colored water and strange alien body parts (use some unusual rubber creature toy), add air filter for bubbles effect.

HAUNTED MANSION EFFECTS:

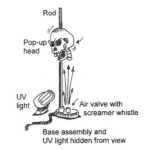

Rod

Pop-up head

UV light

Air valve with screamer whistle

Base assembly and UV light hidden from view

There are several tricks used in the Haunted Mansion of a popular theme park that we'll quickly discuss. Make shrieking heads that pop up for a split second. Attached small ghastly molded heads to a rod about 24" long, with the base and pressured air valve that performs two functions. When a blast of compressed air is piped through a hose to the valve, it creates a loud shriek, and shoots the head up the rod. Since the air blast is so brief, the head quickly drops back out of sight. Paint the head is in ghostly fluorescent colors, and illuminated with UV light.

Another trick is used for the portrait in the parlor entrance, the crystal ball with a woman's animated head inside, a small ghostly image of a woman giving a warning at the end, and the

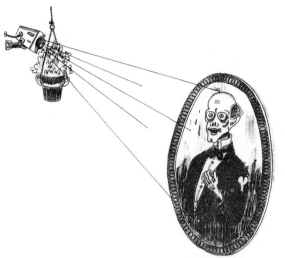

ghoulish animated faces of several inverted busts who are singing in base tone voices to passing guests. These are images that can be projected onto the objects from a hidden VCR projector. You can perform this by projecting the image onto a Styrofoam wig stand, a faceless bust or dummy, or any flat light-colored surface from a hidden video projector position overhead and behind the guest, playing a prerecorded tape on a VCR. Use your camcorder to tape just your face or head, masking the remaining background in black felt (cut hole for head or face).

The ghosts that appear to be seated in your car are actually seen through a reflection in a darkened glass window panel. This effect can be created using the same type of lighting techniques described above with the transformation rooms trick.

Our friend trying to escape the coffin can be made with some plastic prop skeleton hands being pivoted up and down on a mechanized rotating rod assembly. You could also power the hands with the compressed air tracked on rods like the popping heads. If you add a person experienced with mechanical devices and movement, and they have a good imagination, you'll be amazed at what they can fabricate at fairly reasonable prices.

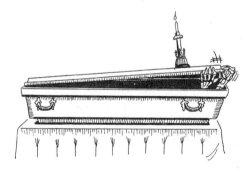

The bending, breathing doors can be made of foam rubber treated with latex paint to resemble wood grain, with a rotating mechanized device attached to the backside of the door to create the bowing motion. Many of these effects can be easily recreated when using prop builders familiar with available materials and mechanized devices used in the trade.

HAUNTED HOUSE IDEAS Tricks to Play

Chapter 2

IMPALED AND LOVIN' IT:

Attaching an impaled corpse to the wall is just okay until you add a little life to it. Hide a small speaker behind the body out of sight, and attach some fine fishing line to the lower jaw. You could even rig up movable glass eyeballs if you really want to spook them. Then hide the actor operating the "Dead Ventriloquist dummy" behind the wall, and get ready for some fun. If you can make small unnoticeable holes, or position a mini video camera to allow the operator to view patrons on a monitor inside the wall a more personalized assault can be made. Have thunder sound effects and lightening from a strobe start the performance off. Great to keep crowds entertained while waiting in line.

HOW ABOUT A LITTLE SNACK:

In this scare you simply position an old refrigerator in an otherwise empty room. Leave the door slightly open (do this by tilting the refrigerator back slightly so the door closes itself, but install a doorstop inside that keeps door open about 1"). Have a light on inside the refrigerator with no other lights on in the room other than a single 48" UV tube to illuminate a white sign that reads, "Open for your treat". Inside the refrigerator have a few cobwebs, the bones of a rack of ribs on an old dirty plate, and a dead rat lying next to the ribs. Have a character dressed in all black lurking in the shadows to step out and grab the shoulder of whomever opens the door, while shouting, "Hey, git outa there mortal."

IT'S FOR YOU:

Have a phone in a room ring. When a patron picks it up have a hidden hose from an air compressor spray them with a sharp burst of air (not in the face). Then simultaneously have a loud sound effect like a truck air horn or amplified scream blare out at the victim. A strobe light may also come on to add to the confusion.

SPARKS ANYONE:

In this scare a heavy metal screen mesh is nailed to the indoor frame over a window. Connect a ground cable between the ground terminal of a charged car battery and the screen. Attach a second cable to the positive terminal of the car battery and the other end of the cable is connected to a metal rod or clamp. Jumper cables can also be used. A costumed character hides behind the old drapes of the window either dressed in all black, or as a rotting corpse. When a patron passes by the window the character scrapes the rod or jumper cable clamp across the screen sending out a surprise shower of sparks from the screen. Use the loud sound effect of a boom to add to the scare. User wears heavy rubber gloves.

FLASH NEWS REPORT:

Have a living room scene with an old 25" screen TV playing and no one else in the room. The TV provides the only light, and it is playing a VHS tape (from a hidden VCR) made earlier of a television show being interrupted by a special news flash. The news announcer claims they are reporting live at the scene of a haunted house where police have tracked down a psychotic serial murderer. The announcer continues by saying the police report there is still a small group of patrons inside unaware of the situation. The murder is inside the house with them armed with a large knife that he just used to stab a convenience store employee. Then an actor in a prison costume brandishing a large knife jumps out from behind the couch lunging at the patrons with one manic scream. Turn on a strobe light to make the situation even more frightening.

CORPSE IN BED:

In a tattered unmade bed have a Character dressed in a skeleton costume lying perfectly still in an awkward pose to look like a prop. The room is only lit by 4' UV fluorescent tubes. Just as the group is leaving the lights go out, then a strobe comes on and the character bounds out of bed toward the patrons rattling a can filled with small rocks on a short stick or sounding a canister air horn.

FINAL IDEAS:

Try a coffin with a hinged back panel, positioned against a fake wall with a secret opening that the coffin back opens into. Attach a skeleton to the back, so when it's opened a costumed figure can take its place using a curtain matching the material of the coffin to cover the opening. The guests enter, and the coffin is open with a wooden stake in the ribs. The tour guide pulls it out to show the guests. The lid of the coffin quickly shuts by itself (rig a fine line), and quickly reopens with a costumed vampire or corpse returned to life. He then leaves the coffin moving out into the guests.

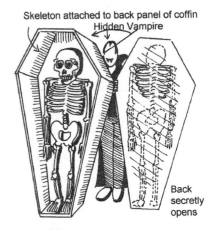

Skeleton attached to back panel of coffin
Hidden Vampire

Back secretly opens

Also you can use three coffins or mummies tombs, two contain props, one with live costumed helper. For added effect have your hidden helper animate parts of the prop figures like a hand twitch, or an arm, foot or leg shift. The narrator walks over to each telling a sordid story about each body swatting the prop with a hard whip from a cane, until he gets to the live corpse that grabs the cane, and comes after the group.

In preparation for the next edition, we'll have our scouts out researching the market to discover the latest and greatest from this rapidly growing Halloween attraction industry. Keep us in mind if you come across a good trick or illusion that we could publish in our next edition. Contact information is listed in the introduction. Once you use a trick, even when the audience can't figure out what was done, the impact of the trick will be significantly reduced if used again the following season. So the objective is to stay original, and rotate new ideas each year to keep your guests off guard. Have fun, practice first, and keep it safe.

Regardless of whether you build or buy, always test and adjust all ideas for your specific haunt conditions.

HAUNTED HOUSE LAYOUT SCENES

The primary difference between this section and the layout scenes sections in the Trick-or-Treaters and Parties chapters, is that the illusions and props get a little larger and more involved. This means either more money invested in buying props, or more time in building props. We won't be describing anything too sophisticated as far as special effects, since these usually also require unique skills and training to perform.

Remember to include ideas from other chapters for your rooms. We have tried to avoid repeating material from those chapters in this section to encourage you to read the entire book, even if you're only interested in producing a haunted house. You'll notice we don't spend much "space" discussing total house layouts. We hope that we have provided enough of the basic guidelines to allow you to apply them to the unique conditions and structure that characterize your house or facility. Oh yes, always remember to take a "head count" of all those going in and coming out of your haunted house. We wouldn't want anyone becoming one of the "props"…

TRANSFORMATION ROOMS:

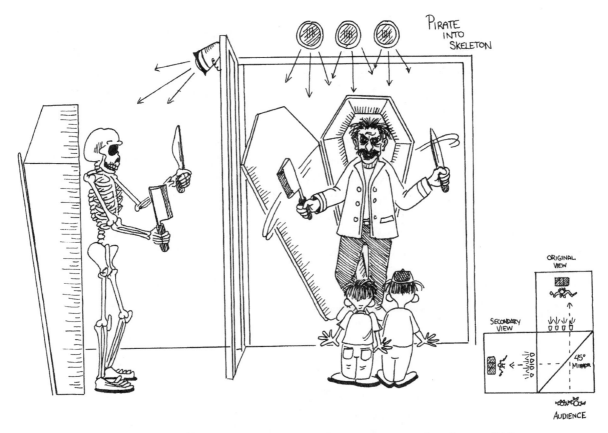

- Often used at carnivals and side shows, three small square rooms forming an "L" pattern are used (see Haunted House Illusions).

- The matching rooms can be used for a variety of illusions where the item in one room turns into the item in a second room, but the audience is only viewing one room while watching the transformation illusion. A large piece of glass helps create the illusion.

- The most popular has been using a woman in one room changing into a caged gorilla (character in costume) positioned in the hidden room, and then after the transformation the gorilla breaks out of its cage (see props chapter), the lights go out, and the gorilla comes after the patrons.

- Change a well dressed man (in suit or tux) into a well dressed corpse or skeleton (in matching clothes).

- Change a vampire in a coffin into a large bat (suspended from ceiling with fine line).

- Change a shackled prisoner into a shackled werewolf who then breaks out of his chains to come after the audience.

- Change a beautiful woman looking into a dressing mirror into an ugly witch.

- Change a mad scientist who drinks a potion into a Mr. Hyde.

WALL OF IMPRESSIONS:

- Create a false wall of either fabric or heavy black plastic sheeting, decorate it to look like the surrounding walls (interior house wall papered, cave, prison stone block, etc.).

- Have characters on the opposite side of the wall making hand and facial impressions while moaning like ghosts. Watch out for punching!

- Use a strobe light on the wall to create even a greater effect.

- You can also create a wall of shadows where you use a cloth wall that is dyed in print of the wall's pattern. Have the narrator tell a story about the history of the house involved with this very hall. At the climax, the sound of thunder and flash of lighting causes the hallway lights to go out. The costumed characters on the opposite side of the wall, with a bright light behind them to cast their shadows onto the fabric or paper wall, go into a pantomime of a pre-planned skit, like a mad man trying to stab a woman, or what ever chilling tale the narrator spins. Keep the characters close to the wall for crisper shadows (see Haunted House tricks)

- Another possibility is to have a hallway wall panel quickly slide open to expose an ugly character's head in makeup or mask. Light the character from below with a flash light (have character wear a black turtle neck shirt). This can also be triggered at the climax of a story, lights go out, etc. The story may be of the house's previous owner losing his head to the knife of a jealously crazed wife in the very spot that we are standing 100 years ago tonight, and his head has been seen floating in this hallway looking for his body.

- A final possibility of this theme is for the narrator to tell the story of an evil magician who lived in the house, casting a spell over the house on his death bed. This spell announces that anyone trespassing through this secret hallway will meet with a terrible fate. Then again, (camera strobe flashes) lighting causes the lights to go out, and a strobe light illuminates the hallway to show a half dozen ugly bloody hands and arms reaching through the wall out to the tour group. To do this, use a patterned fabric, paper, or plastic sheeting that can have small round flaps cut unnoticeably from the front, just big enough for an arm, which can be secured shut with Velcro® tabs.

- Note: Be sure to use a railing or some type of barrier to prevent the patrons from direct reach of the wall, but be as close as possible.

ROOM OF CONFUSION:

- In this room all the furniture of what you would expect to find in an old abandoned house is nailed down to either the ceiling or a wall
- Choose an interior room, kitchen, study, living room, dining room, library, a den, a bedroom, or even a bathroom
- Use fine fishing line and motors to create movement of a rocking chair, have a clock with the hands attached to a small motor to speed or reverse their movement, have a bone swinging as a pendulum
- Have costumed figures dressed like corpses sitting in the furniture (secure with fine fishing line from underneath)
- Use blue rotating beacons or strobe lights to give the illusion of movement
- Have the tour group walk across the ceiling for effect
- For additional confusion, build a false floor supported in the corners by rope to give a swaying effect when walked across, tilt the floor about 20 degrees, or use thick upholstery foam rubber on the floor.

CLOSET SURPRISE:

- Have a closest that is accessed from a hall? Here is a great hair-raiser. Have the door almost closed, but have a rod attached to the inside so a character can make the door slowly open a little, then close to attract attention of the touring group.

- Inside the closet, the doorway is bricked up except for a 12"x12" barred window (and a small hole to allow for control rod on door), looking like the closet was converted into a prison.

- When a curious patron asks the narrator what is behind the door, the narrator says they don't know, because no one has ever been able to get that door open.

- Have a very faint flickering light (use a low watt candle bulb) behind the brick wall to encourage the curious to look inside.

- Release tension on rod to allow someone to open the door (rod is attached at the bottom inside corner out of view).

- On the other side of the wall stands a helper waiting for someone to look into the window. When someone does, they release a mounted springboard with a head attached to the end that makes a loud slam noise, and puts a corpse face right up to the bars (see Haunted House tricks section)

- An alternative version is for a costumed character in a corpse mask or makeup to quickly put their face up to the window, with a flashlight under it for light, and yell at the same instant.

- Lighting and sound can really support the surprise element of this trick. Your brick wall can be painted cardboard, wooden siding, plywood, etc. You can also use various interior false brick surfaces.

SEANCE OF THE DEAD:

- ☠ The patrons look into a very dimly lit room furnished in a old Victorian parlor decorum, with a round table and five of your characters, dressed normally, seated around it as the centerpiece of attention in the room.

- ☠ The seance leader is reciting some odd rehearsed dialog used to conjure up the dead

- ☠ Have oddity props setting around like you might expected to find in some half-baked phony seance master's place of business. This might include small stuffed animals, a Ouija board, a glass eyeball on a display stand, a severed hand in an open box with red felt lining, etc., get creative, look in some books for ideas

- ☠ Have the seance leader stop abruptly screaming out, "Oh no, I've said the wrong incantation, we're all doomed!" Then, the lights go out for a few seconds as you hear the hideous screams of the seance table attendees.

- ☠ The tour guide finally gets his flashlight to work, and shines it in on the party sitting at the table, each very still, and slightly slumped over now.

- ☠ All is quiet, because all the members have joined the spirits they were hoping to visit, and are turned into either skeletons or corpses. Characters stay dressed in original clothing, but quickly slip on masks and fake hands, or substitute corpse props when the lights are out. Use a background CD or Tape to cover the sounds made when the lights are out, the character's screams aren't enough to cover all sounds.

- ☠ Have the corpse seance master (made up to look like a skeleton) slowly raise her head, and ask if the tour group would like to join in on a little seance.

NEVER-ENDING HALLWAY:

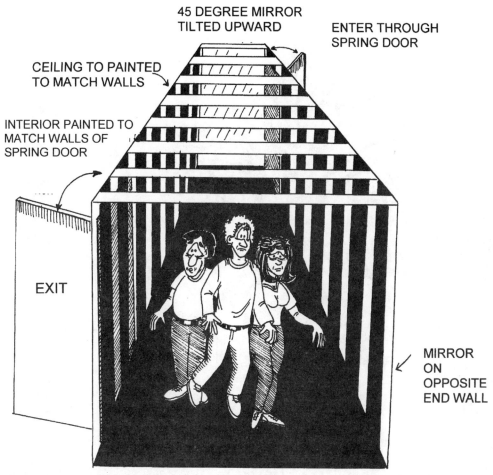

- ☠ This illusion has been popular at carnival fun houses for years.
- ☠ You'll need a hallway that is at least 15" long, the longer the better.
- ☠ Paint the walls and ceiling flat black, have nothing hanging on the walls, then paint either white or bright yellow stripes about 2"-3" wide every 12" from the floor, straight up the wall, across the ceiling, and back down the opposite wall to create a caged appearance. Also paint doorways into the hallway black with stripes.
- ☠ Use either 3' fluorescent tube type black lights on the ceiling or a couple of strobe lights pointed at either side of the wall to minimize distractions.
- ☠ Have doorways open from the side walls, and large mirrors completely covering each end of the hallway wall. So, when walking down the hall the patron is always looking into a mirror which creates the endless hall illusion.
- ☠ For more disorienting effect, install a false floor that leans at a 20 slant.
- ☠ The narrator explains that this is the hall of nightmares, warning that some patrons never make it out.

HAUNTED FOREST:

- ☠ This room may be a total change from the rest of the rooms format, it can even be set up in a room inside, or outside as the group leaves through the back door. Regardless, inside or out, use it as a final attraction. Use old dead tree limbs, bushes, leaves, and brush to create a haunted forest.

- ☠ Make or buy a couple of realistic looking tree costumes. Position characters inside to stand very still as the group approaches. Have bats fly through the air suspended on fine lines.

- ☠ Make or buy a couple of costumes that look like an old rock, bush, or tree stump. Use upholstery foam-rubber cut to shape. Paint in a brown, black, or gray base, glued to a totally black costume. Then glue bark chips, mulch, leaves, or whatever it takes to make it look natural (get suggestions from a local university drama department).

- ☠ The narrator acts like the tour is over, thanks everyone for coming, then turns and leaves, as the forest comes to life, turn on strobes for additional confusion.

- ☠ Use a variety of outdoor life props like owls with lighted eyes, bats, spiders, and snakes. Also, paint up wooden signs saying things like "I'd turn back if I were you," "No feeding the trees," "Pick my fruit, and I'll take your arms!," "Trees-R-Us," and "Trespassers will be eaten."

CEMETERY:

- ☠ This is a similar setting to the forest as far as the outdoor effects. Set up outside or in a room with a false floor covered in grass, high weeds, lots of dead leaves, with a few lifelike prop trees, bushes, and many headstones.

- ☠ Have several characters lying in shallow graves, out of sight, covered with mulch and leaves. They should wear various styles of old tattered formal burial dress and corpse masks, or makeup.

- ☠ For props, use painted foam-rubber for old fence gatePlace an owl in a tree, bats hanging on fine fishing line, headstone out of painted wood or Styrofoam pieces with comical epitaphs like "Here rests Fred, walked the earth until he was dead," "In this hole lies the prankster Gene, found out too late how his wife's real mean," etc. (see Chapter 5 Props to add to the Horror).

- ☠ If indoors, make a moon out of a swag globe lamp on a dimmer switch turned down very low. Cut a hole in a facing wall and have a large white globe bulb sticking out, turn low with a dimmer switch.

CEMETERY CONT.:

☠ Have the narrator telling a story of how the prior owner of this house, back a hundred and eighty years ago, was believed to be a witch. She was accused of luring young men into her house by transforming herself into a beautiful maiden, and then poisoning them for parts needed for her black magic potions. It was rumored that one night an angery crowd mobbed the house to burn her at the stake for her crimes. She ran out the back door to escape, carrying her most powerful potions, but she tripped over a bone sticking up from a shallow unmarked grave of one of her victims, spilling all the evil potions over the graves of her victims. These victims immediately came back to life. Up out of the ground in their decayed state, they captured the witch, and pulled her back down into the soft ground to join them. It's rumored that whenever the moon is full on Halloween night these ghouls come back to life looking for yet other "playmates" to join them.

☠ Use a loud sound effect of thunder, and a double flash for lightning from two camera strobes.

☠ After the story, have the ghouls coming out of the ground for another victim, with the tour guide leaving the group running ahead screaming, or the tour guide removes a mask of a normal person to show a corpse face, laughing hideously chanting "Why you're just in time for dinner!"

☠ You may want to flip on the strobe lights at this point, to add to the confusion.

☠ If you have a large tree, hide one of your helpers up in it, they can drop a skeleton or ghost marionette in the middle of the bedlam. (watch out for pint-sized lumber jacks toting saws).

☠ Have at least one costumed character headless, staggering around feeling for a head.

☠ For a real shocker have one of your helpers act like they are on the tour, then they get caught by one of the corpses, and dragged off screaming (Don't use a female, some nutty male patron may try to save her).

EVIL LABORATORY:

- ☠ There are a variety of stunts that can be staged, but whatever the stunt, the scene should be decorated to look like an old laboratory.

- ☠ For props, use an old dark wooden table as the center piece. Have old cobweb-covered shelves filled with beakers, test tubes, flasks, jars of chemicals, large clear jars with human body parts pickling in fluid, skulls, bones, rats, or a shabby light fixture with a cheap circular metal shade hanging from the ceiling.

- ☠ Larger props could include a skeleton in a cage or shackled to the wall, two large transformation boxes (see Chapter 1 Tricks to Play on Trick-or-Treaters), a character costumed as a gorilla in a cage, with rubber inner tube bars to allow for escape.

- ☠ One scene has the mad scientist character mixing a special experiment (vinegar, baking soda, and red food coloring), he acts like he is about to drink it while laughing hideously. The lights go out, in the dark he quickly puts an ugly mask on, and as the tour guide shines a flashlight onto the mad scientist, he has been transformed into a deformed ghoul or monster. He then starts to growl, coming toward the group when the tour guide's flashlight batteries fail, and the room goes dark again.

- ☠ Another scene uses the table for a surgery victim, parts that are being operated on are hidden in holes in the table, and replaced by prop body parts. If the character's torso is being operated on, or if you use a pendulum swinging overhead slicing into the torso, the character is hidden under the table with only head or appendages stick out, while the victim is flailing around wildly (see Chapter 1 Tricks to Play on Trick-or-Treaters). The mad surgeon then shouts out, "This operation is taking way too long.," and reaches for a large prop ax, as he swings the ax down the light go out, there is a sick slashing chop, and the character flips drops of water in the dark onto the tour group, like splattering blood.

☠ Another scene is where the scientist captures a rat, spider, fly, or something else nasty that you have a large costume to represent. He puts it into one of the transformation boxes, made out of a painted refrigerator box, and closes the door. He then steps into the other box shouting out before closing the door, "We shall now be electronically atomized and transported between vectorizers." The door is closed, the lights go out, a strobe comes on, sound effects come on making electrical sparking sounds, colored lights on the boxes flash on, and then all goes quiet as the door of the box with the creature pops open with a puff of fire and smoke (see magician's hand flasher in Chapter 1 Tricks to Play on Trick-or-Treaters), and the scientist comes out with the head and hands of the creature that was supposed to be transported.

☠ Another scene may find the scientist trying to get the caged ape to participate in his experiment by poking a beaker of the elixir into the cage to drink. The ape finally has had enough, escapes from his cage, knocks the scientist down, out of sight, behind the cloth covered table, and acts like he rips off his head. Holding up the prop head, the angry ape proceeds to start out after the audience.

☠ A final scene could be a body shop with several tables containing bodies in various stages of repair. The room is as picture, with an overhead sign reading "Joe's Body Shop" and boxes with spare parts. Sign on the boxes identify the contents of each part bin (hands, heads, feet). Have body mechanic characters using power tools, like an auto shop, busily putting people together. Then have them stop, one at a time, and stare at the tour group. Once all have stopped and it's quiet, one calls out, "Wow, more spare parts.," and comes after the group with a gas-powered chain saw (without blade) or electric saw (for rooms with poor venting).

HAUNTED ATTIC:

☠ This room is obviously used only if the house has an upstairs, preferably a real attic.

☠ Light the room using 3' flourescent black light, or blue colored bulbs.

☠ This one is fun and easy to stock with props, because it can include old junk that people often throw out or practically give away at yard sales. Get creative. Build a bird skeleton to put in an old bird cage and paint it with luminous paint to glow under black light.

☠ Have a large old trunk positioned in the middle of the room with a hole cut from either underneath or hidden from behind, with a dryer vent hose feeding into the trunk. The other end of the vent pipe should be in another room, out of sounds' reach. This will allow a helper to talk into the pipe and sound like they are the boy's spirit in the trunk.

☠ Have the narrator tell a story about a little boy who was playing hide-and-seek with his family at a family reunion held in this house over 100 years ago to this day. "The boy accidentally locked himself in the trunk while trying to hide there, and never escaped. One day, several years later, his shriveled body was found in that very trunk. His ghost is supposed to still haunt the attic each anniversary night of the family reunion, which happens to be tonight!"

☠ The boy's voice then seems to be coming from the trunk asking for someone to let him out. The tour guide asks if anyone is willing to open the chest. Then, wait for the pop-up surprise.

☠ Have the chest rigged with a an ugly corpse on a springboard that when the lid is opened, pops up out of the chest (see Capter 1 Tricks to Play on Trick-or-Treaters), have another helper either scream or turn on a sound effect.

☠ Another twist is to have a costumed corpse character climb up out of the trunk (A false bottom, and a hole in the floor with a ladder to allow the character to climb up through the trunk is required).

☠ A final, less frightening, effect is to have the narrator tell a different story about how a mad taxidermist was rumored to have lured trick-or-treaters into his house on Halloween, and added them to the collection he kept up in this attic. The narrator laughs, and says how there are also rumors that the children's spirits still haunt the attic. Paint eyes on the walls in luminous paint. For this routine, have a bright light on in the attic when the group enters to charge the eyes. When the Narrator turns out the lights, the glowing spirit eyes cover the walls. An alternative for the glowing-eyes effect is having a false wall with holes for eyes cut, and a bright light from behind lights the holes when the room light is turned out.

SPACE LAB:

- The room is designed to resemble a futuristic space lab.

- Use aluminum foil to cover the walls. Paint yard drain tubing silver. Drape dryer vent tubing overhead. Use lots of mock control panels with flashing lights. In the center of the ceiling attach a large red covered rotating beacon light (available at Radio Shack), and car alarm siren (left off until alarm turns on).

- If you have access to any computers with monitors (especially 17" screen) have them on some animated screen saver that looks like it is monitoring some function. Alternatively, have characters running some graphic or spreadsheet monitoring programs.

- Have the characters dressed in space suits.

- Use a variety of strange looking prop creatures in bird and hamster cages (see if a pet store will loan them to you, particularly a real large cage).

- Have tubes coming out of large jars with colored water (use dry ice for effect).

- Have a large refrigerator box painted either silver or black, with a door cut into the side and barred window cut in the front up high, so you can't see inside (use a bicycle inner-tube for bars). Clamp auto jumper cables onto silver rods sticking out of the top of the box leading to a transformer prop. Attach a large red or yellow light bulb sticking out of the top of the box on a dimmer switch to adjust brightness from within.

- Have "Danger High Voltage" signs painted in large red letters on each side of the box.

- The head scientist explains that the crew has captured a violent and deadly creature that requires constraint using thousands of volts of electricity to keep subdued. If they lost power, this creature would come crashing out of that restraint cylinder like it was a popcorn box, and we'd all be in serious trouble.

- Have other space costumed characters sitting at monitoring stations busy at work watching their screens, turning adjustment knobs and writing down data.

- Have a sound effect come on making a loud snapping crack of electricity. At the same time have one of the monitoring station characters set off either a camera strobe, a magician's hand flasher, a "Jacob's Ladder," or any other special effect that can safely make sparks fly.

- Have the costumed figure inside the box set the siren off, and turn the overhead beacon flashing on, the head scientist yells out, "Oh no, we've lost our main power generator," while the light on the box is flickered, then gradually dimmed out

- Then have all lights go out except a strobe light and the overhead beacon, while the character hidden inside the box begins making hideous noises, and pounds his way out of the door of the box.

- Then have all lights go out and all characters scream

- After a few seconds have the lights come on, and the crew is gone. Have all the space crew sneak out in the dark through a hidden side door (paint luminous dots on floor to lead to the door for characters to follow in dark). Have the monster standing there, and say, "Yummm.... Space fries, my favorite."

- Another effect would be to have a fog machine (these can be rented, but buy it when you can afford it because of poor availability around Halloween). Have the fogger behind the box or console, and turn it on when the sparks begin to fly.

- If you have a sound effects machine, have it play a sound effect that pulsates at an increasing pitch louder and louder to add to the atmosphere

HALLOWEEN HOSPITAL:

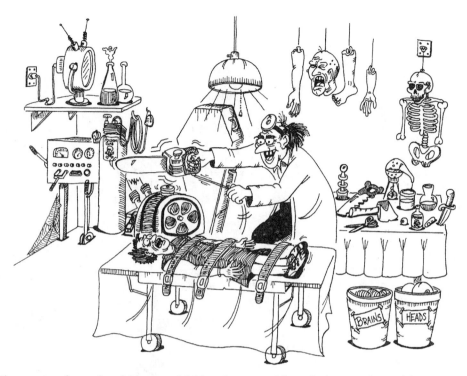

- The centerpiece should be an old blood covered hospital operating table. You can use an old fold-out cot and fabricate taller legs for it. For trick effects, make a table with the side facing out decorated to look like an operating table with a bloody sheet hanging to the floor to mask character underneath.

- Use a dismembered dummy or create that impression with a live character sticking some body parts out of hole in the bed. Have a surgeon hacking off parts for crude effect. You can even use a rubber squeeze bulb with hidden tubing to squirt out colored water or fake blood mixture (watch out for staining). Probably not a good idea to serve pizza at this party

- Body parts, body parts, body parts everywhere, hanging on walls, in jars of water to pickle, on the floor.

- Large bladed knives, axes, saws, hatchets etc. can be hung on the wall as instruments. Use pegboard or an old set of shelves to hang instruments. Dress up the scene with other lab type props like clear beakers with colored water and use dry ice for effect. Your character can start a chainsaw without chain for effect (use electric-powered chain saw indoors).

- Use a shop light with a homemade shade for overhanging light. Light with low watt colored bulbs or even black light bulb.

- Create flashing colored lights sticking out of boxes made to look like diagnostic instruments. Add shiny knobs, levers, gauges, wires, pole antennas, and switches.

- For background sounds, use tape or CD of moans, groans and screams from Halloween tape.

- Hang a net bag with human bones and skulls with a sign "Mistakes" on the front.

TORTURE CHAMBER:

- The atmosphere must be cold and dark. So, drape walls with either paper or sheets painted to resemble stone, rock, or concrete block. Include shackles and bars for prison cells. Build walls behind bars to give 3D effect to view imprisoned dummies, skeletons, props and characters.
- Review the illustrations in Chapter 5 Props To Add to the Horror for ideas of various types of torture equipment to build, buy, or… borrow from your in-laws, parents, or a friend!!!
- Scatter skeletons or corpse-like dummies shackled to the walls, rubber skull, bones, and large rats generously around the floor
- Suspend large black spiders in cobwebs in the corners, and hang bats from the ceiling using fine fishing line or thread.
- Have a costumed character or dummy to look like executioner/torturer.
- Light with very low lighting either hidden from view or coming from barred windows of fabricated wall, or behind props.
- Make a chopping block. Have the character or dummy lay head on block, executioner swings down ax, lights go off, flip drops of water onto guests like it's blood. Then, turn lights back on.
- Create special effects of severing limbs and squirting blood (see Chapter 2 Haunted House Ideas tricks).

HAUNTED HOUSE:

☠ Everything left in the room must be made to look old and abandoned. Cover windowpanes from the outside using black plastic to prevent light from coming in. Drapes should be replaced with old sheets made to look like drapes.

☠ Ghosts floating in closets or down halls, not just out in the open, give the best effect, (see Chapter 1 "Tricks for Trick-or-Treaters").

☠ Set a full-length mirror against back closet wall with the door open to really scare them with something unpredictable and ugly. Use a Halloween tape or CD with ghostly sound effects.

☠ Have rubber hands coming out of the walls. This can be accomplished by using an opening or fashioning a false wall with a hole and have a character's hand sticking out in motion, you can purchase motorized motion hands for a price at Halloween prop stores.

☠ Use plenty of cob webbing, large rubber spiders, bats, bugs, and rats.

☠ Build a small table with a hole large enough to use for either a "thing -type" body part in a box that can be opened by the guests for a surprise or popped open by the character under the table. Use an old table cloth and make the box small dark and old looking.

☠ On false walls, can hang portraits with open eyeholes so that characters behind the wall can look through.

☠ Suspend objects from the ceiling using fine fishing line. These can be candlestick holders, small lamps, knickknacks, or other desktop/household items.

☠ Hang a skeleton in a closet. Have the door open itself. Then close it. When reopened, the skeleton can be replaced by a ghostly costumed character (see Chapter 2 Haunted House).

HALLOWEEN PARTY FUN

Try Expanding Your "Creative Spirit"...   Exhaust a Notion...   or Just Harness Your Imagination

This chapter is designed to help give your party real "spirit." Parties are prime opportunities to have fun playing a few tricks, try wacky Halloween food recipes, or play silly games. Lighting and sound effects are also good mood-setters. Be sure that you read the chapters on scaring trick-or-treaters, and the haunted house chapter for additional ideas, since those won't be repeated in this chapter.

Decorations used for parties vary widely. You can go with a light atmosphere by selecting party decorations from a party shop, or you can go a step further by having a prop party. Here you will create a variety of non-animated scenes in various rooms or corners of rooms to inspire a haunting atmosphere using props and figures. This is a more expensive technique to decorating a party, but provides a spookier atmosphere.

Planning a theme for your party can help your decisions for layout scenes, costumes, food, and any tricks or effects. The more popular choices include a spooky haunted house theme, a frightful mad scientist theme with various mutilated bodies and parts (not our first choice for a party with food and drink), a specialty theme like space-futuristic, devices of punishment & torture (you can inject a little humor with this one), or maybe a theme on phobias (trains, heights, water, spiders & snakes, etc.). The objective is to be creative and have fun. Do not take it all on your shoulders alone seek out a friend for help.

TRICKS TO PLAY AT PARTIES

EXPLODING BALLOONS:

Theater Effects sells a system that allows you to attach little wires to balloons called "squibs" that detonate the balloons when activated with a small electrical charge. They even sell lights that can fit inside the balloon. Consider filling balloons with confetti

for effect, or if outside, water, Gelatin, shaving cream, or whipped cream. Position the balloons where people might stand or sit to talk, near food, or even in a bathroom. You can use cheap bell wire purchased from an electronics store, connected to either one 9-volt battery, or an inexpensive battery pack kit that holds several AA batteries. Set the charge with a small switch wired into the system or touch wires directly to the batteries.

With a little pre-wiring, there are hundreds of different gags that this effect can exploit. Create a quiet time to explode a balloon, like at the climax of a ghost story. You could even have a pressure sensitive switch under a favorite candy or treat with a sign by it saying, "do not eat." If someone picks it up, "Boom-Boom-Boom," three balloons explode. Hide switches under seat cushions or floor mats.

You can also detonate balloons using wireless switches. Even use an infrared switch from a garage door opener. Get creative and think up many more.

FLOATING GHOSTS:

Perform another trick by filling large balloons with helium, and attaching a lightweight white cloth as a ghost body heavy enough to cause each balloon head to hover at about 5' off the ground. Tie a 6'-7' black thread to a small opened paper clip (so it looks like a hook), and attach the other end to the base of the ghost. Now try to secretly hook the back of a guest so the ghost follows it hot pursuit.

GRABBING FURNITURE:

Make a costume to look just like a stuffed chair or recliner, only the back of the chair is a hidden helper heady to grab the next unsuspecting weary guest that sits down. You can also do this trick by simply making the costume out of an old slipcover. The helper sits on top of an old chair hidden under the slipcover. You can find cheap used furniture at garage sales and thrift shops.

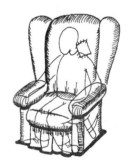

FLASHING SURPRISE:

Make a sign and tape it onto the bathroom medicine cabinet door reading "Please keep door closed, very personal. Inside, rig a switch that activates when the door is opened. Attach a car siren, a powerful strobe flash, an emergency warning horn, etc., and in addition, fill the cabinet with popped popcorn.

SPOOKY FOOD:

Favorites here include the gelatin molds you can buy at companies like Brainstorms or other companies listed in the reference chapter. They have molds for a hand, a heart, and a brain. I have also seen face molds, so you could add a head to your collection. They recommend using peach gelatin for flesh tone, and a good French vanilla for a brain.

Use peeled grapes, green olives, or jarred white onions for eyes. Use candy corn for teeth and cotton candy for hair. Use cauliflower, cottage cheese or pasta for brains, and use liver for...well, use your imagination. You can cut ears out of baked cheese pizza, make fingers out of breaded fish sticks, and carve noses out of apples or pears.

Look through a recipe book using a little imagination. Each course can use simple adjustments to make the food item frighteningly questionable. The main meat can be formed hamburger, the vegetable, dyed mashed potatoes, spaghetti, or squash. The salad should use a variety of unusual additions, and desert can be uniquely formed with died cookie dough, or molded cakes with colored icings and toppings using coconut, peanut butter, cherry sauce, and many more.

BOB FOR APPLES OR WHATEVER:

Set up the traditional tub with water and apples. In this instance, however, add a little dry ice to the water creating a foggy challenge. To protect from burns from the ice, submerge the ice in a plastic net produce bag. Use potatoes, small water balloons, rubber body parts, or even snapping turtles instead of apples for added effect.

HEADS UP

For a real shocker, make a small table with a sheet of plywood attaching inexpensive prefabricated legs or use a couple of folding chairs. Cut a hole large enough for a head, then buy a paper table cloth and cut a matching hole. Use several decorative paper plates to create a plate collar for the helper. Then, find a helper dumb enough to volunteer to let you have fun decorating their face with a combination of whipped cream, icing, fruit, candy, a cake or whatever. Use a make-up latex head cap to protect hair. For an added touch, circle the neck with gelatin cubes. When guests are invited over to the table to snack, or to celebrate a fictitious birthday, invite someone to cut the cake (offer a Rubber bladed knife). Just as the guest is ready to cut, the centerpiece comes to life with an ear-shattering shriek.

68

SPOOKY SEANCE:

This is always a fun party trick, and has dozens of
variations that can be combined for a more
memorable effect. The group works best with 6 or
less, but a larger group can sit in a circle on the floor.
The mysterious build-up is important for atmosphere.
The seance leader should be some unrecognized
character costumed to look like an old gypsy with a
patch over one eye. The seance may use a crystal ball
with special lighting effects (see Chapter 7 Props) as
a centerpiece if desired. Use some of these tricks
during a session held in a dark room:

- ☠ Have a sound system set up with speakers
  hidden in various corners of the room. With a
  multiple channel amp, have a hidden helper
  return from the dead, using various voices for
  different ghosts.

- ☠ Project ghosts onto a wall using a slide
  projector or super8 projector hidden in
  another room. Try reflecting the image off
  one or two mirrors to help hide the projection. Have background sounds of wind to
  cover up the projector noises. With a little skill you can tape or photograph just the
  face of a person sticking through a black background for a truly spooky image in your
  projection.

- ☠ Make something sail across the room with the object
  attached to a very fine overhead line, while
  controlling it by a drawstring (black thread) from a
  hidden helper. Flying objects can include a small
  ghost made from a handkerchief painted with
  luminous paint, or an object owned by the deceased,
  like a pocket watch, a hat, jewelry, etc. For added
  effect, have the helper pull the guideline down before
  turning on the lights, so as not reveal the trick.

- ☠ Lower a ghostly corpse or spirit prop from a second
  story window in front of one of the seance room
  windows using a fine fishing line and a rapid draw
  reel and rod. Have the figure painted in fluorescent
  colors, and shine a UV light down from overhead. A
  severed head or cheesecloth over a torso corpse prop
  looks the best for this. Practice the night before to learn the best lighting and prop
  movement and positioning.

- ☠ Rulers under the sleeves of the seance leader allow him to keep his hands on the table
  and raise the table for another great illusion.

- ☠ As an angry response from the dead, use 2-3 closely timed camera flashes, and thunder
  sound effects produced from a source near an outside window.

☠ Have a seance, with the medium asking the spirit one embarrassing question about each guest, with the spirit voice returning comical answers. Tell the spirits to single out the person who failed to wash their hands after using the restroom, and explode a balloon by that person, with just wire and a 9-volt battery near the balloon.

☠ Have the medium join hands with all, and send a mild electrical shock with novelty low volt DC electric shocker device or small transformer at just the right moment.

☠ With a foot pedal switch, have an air hose hidden under the table pointing up the legs of a guest used when asking the spirit for a sign of their presence.

There are dozens more tricks that you can find in select magic books that specialize in seance illusions, or create additional ideas by brainstorming with several creative friends.

ADULT PARTY GAMES:

There is a variety of good books in the reference chapter that cover this topic, like "The Great Halloween Book." Some of these games can be a little corny, but add a few imaginative twists. Offer some unusual, unique, and sought after prizes that can be somewhat inexpensive, but hard to find. (Look in unusual catalogs from companies listed in our reference chapter). The competition and interest will heat up, and can make for a memorable evening as people seek certain gifts in which they have an interest. Just watch the alcohol intake levels, so things do not get out of hand.

"Haunted Snitch" is one fun game. Each guest is to bring an unusual seasonal spooky gift that costs less than $5 or $10. Uniquely wrap each gift, and place it in the center of the floor. Before the party, cook up a large bowl of cold spaghetti, and buy a bag of fake plastic eyes. Using fingernail polish, paint numbers from 1 up to double the number of guests that bring gifts onto the eyeballs. Mix the eyeballs in with the spaghetti. A witchly host walks around to each of the guests, making two rounds. The host offers each guest a chance to reach in and select one eyeball out of a bowl. Tell the players the bowl contains all that is left of your last visitor). Once each guest has selected two eyeballs (after two rounds), the game begins.

The guest holding number one starts first. They select a gift from the pile, and open it. Then, the guest holding number two takes a turn by either taking an opened gift away from someone, or selecting one unopened. If a person already has a gift, they can either keep it, trade it for another opened gift, or return it to the pile and select a new gift if there are any new gifts left. Allow each player to hold only one gift. This routine continues until all eyeballs have been played. There really are no winners.

MISC. TRAPS:

There is a variety of trick traps that can be set around the party for unsuspecting guests. One explodes confetti onto the subject when they open a cupboard or door. To promote curiosity Hang a sign reading, "Please, keep out no matter what."

You can also set a cap exploding device under anything to get a real shock when the item is picked up (use food, a book titled "Nude Family Photos," or whatever to entice the person).

You can use a shocking pen or lighter that gives a mild but startling shock when used.

You can fire a hand held confetti cannon, set out some dribble glasses, or try dehydrated worms in a drink. Go to a joke / trick store for additional ideas.

Use a jackhammer plate. Hide the jack hammer plate under a rug beside the punch bowl with a sign warning "Caution, punch is highly spiked." Then watch the fun.

There is a great assortment of plans to build everything from a marionette floating ghost (called a Flying Crank Ghost) to pop-up monsters from a trash can (Trash Can Trauma) at the web site for the Halloween-L archives http://www.calweb.com/~bertino/halloween.html.

Also, get ideas from Halloween prop and costume web sites and catalogs listed in chapter 8.

PARTY SCENES:

In this section we'll describe haunting layout scenes that will "deaden up" any party. Our primary objective is to stimulate your imagination so you can build on our suggestions. The advantage to you is to see how this chapter can reduce the planning time by providing a foundation of scenery ideas to build on. As we've mentioned before, party supplies can quickly add up, so consider making some of your decorations or props, and possibly borrowing a few as well (but not from a mortuary, cemetery, or hospital please).

Each section that follows simply describes a scene that may be the centerpiece of the party. We don't go into the details of streamers, wall hangings, balloons and other party supply decorations, since most of that kind of stuff is a ...

FUNERAL PARTY:

☠ The centerpiece will be a long dark cloth-draped table with a coffin resting on top.

☠ Position 3 - 4 dummies costumed as corpses seated around the coffin showing their respects, and one dummy nicely dressed giving the eulogy.

☠ Have another table set up on an opposite wall with hors d'oeuvres produced to give a ghastly effect (Deviled eggs with olive eyeballs, peach gelatin hands, etc.).

☠ Use low watt colored light bulbs for lighting (preferably orange and yellow).

☠ Have solemn organ music playing in the background.

☠ Decorate generously with cob webs, spiders, and other large bugs.

☠ Make certain all windows are covered in black, have a skeleton dressed in work clothes with shovel in corner as the grave digger.

☠ Host and Hostess are obviously dressed like someone out of the Addams Family®.

☠ Have a costumed funeral director taking coffin measurements of the guests.

WITCH'S PARTY:

☠ The centerpiece will be a large witch's caldron of bubbling brew (see Chapter 5 Props) with dry ice in warm colored water for effect.

☠ Position a table near the cauldron, and build some shabby old shelves out of scrap lumber from the scrap cart at your local large hardware/building supplies retailer or scrap pile of a home construction site. Then paint your home-built masterpiece black or dark gray.

☠ Make spooky labels of grotesque ingredients, and put them over the labels of boxes, cans, and jars of normal food supplies (bat wings, toad lips, eye of newt, lizard tongues). If you can use your computer's word processor select a spooky font of at least 14 point, and print on yellowed or gray paper to look old.

☠ Buy or make a couple 18th century straw brooms to lean against the wall, then distribute a generous share of cobwebs, rubber bats, spiders, rats, etc.

☠ Use orange bulbs in lamps or strobes.

☠ Use general Halloween sound effects tape or CD.

☠ Borrow a couple of black cats. Find a large old book, and re-title it "Spells." Place a large rubber frog on floor dressed in a doll-sized costume and tell the guests this was a rude trick-or-treater.

MONSTER BASH:

☠ The theme here is to use popular movie monsters represented as either costumed dummies or characters.

☠ The Mummy can be resting in a decorative Egyptian coffin made out of a large appliance box, cardboard, paper, wood, etc. It can be made from a dummy wrapped in either cloth bandage wrap, toilette paper, or painted newspaper using paper-maché paste.

☠ The Frankenstein monster can be strapped to a large elevated table top with cables leading to the huge fork switch. The switch can be attached to the front of a generator made from a refrigerator box, decorated with lights and switches. The monster is either a dummy or character costumed, masked, or made-up.

☠ Illuminate each monster scene with strobe lights.

☠ Place dry ice in a tub of water for fog.

☠ Other monsters include Phantom of the Opera, the Creature, Wolfman, The Hunchback, etc.

NIGHTMARE MANIA:

Heights

Water

Dogs or other animals

Trains

Dark Closets

☠ Use your own imagination on this one. What's your worst nightmare? Hanging from the edge of a cliff? Being followed by a strange man? Being chased by some type of animal? Trying to breathe under water? A train coming at you in the dark? Doing your taxes?

☠ For a train make tracks out of half sections of yard timbers and rails out of sections of silver painted 2" x 4"s. Hang spotlight about 6' up in a darkened hall or closet. Use tape or CD of an approaching train for sound effects.

☠ Create a little scene for each nightmare, check with friends or family for other ideas, or make some up. Use the ones that will look scariest in a scene can be made to look realistic.

☠ Lighting should be eerie using strobe lights, color wheels, and other unusual lighting that can create confusion, you can often find these at some of the popular novelty stores.

COSTUMES AND MASKS

Okay, so you're wondering, "What can this guy tell me about costumes and masks that I don't already know from a lifetime of Halloweens?" Well, based on reports we've received describing what you have worn for past Halloween celebrations, I'd say plenty.

In this section, we'll bombard you with hundreds of ideas, so you won't find yourself sitting on the end of the bed in your underwear an hour before the big neighborhood Halloween party thinking blankly, "What am I going to be this year?" If you can't find something here, then don't get off the end of the bed.

After reading this chapter, you shouldn't need to spend hours browsing the stores to decide what to wear this Halloween. By performing our short self-analysis, you should know just what to be. Then, visit the stores or their web sites to find costumes and prices, or make your own by applying the tips and instructions we provide. Our basic objective is to help you quickly, painlessly, and effortlessly select the perfect Halloween costume for your specific personality, budget, targeted use, and local state laws.

CONSIDERATIONS WHEN SELECTING A COSTUME:

If you review the follow considerations before making your final choice of costume or mask, you should be 100% more comfortable and satisfied.

THINGS TO CONSIDER:

Components: A costume is a composition of up to three of the following four possible elements: Masks, Makeup, Clothes, and Accessories.

Comfort: If you plan to wear this thing for a couple of hours, you may consider:

- When wearing a mask instead of make-up, the mask selected allows you and your skin to breathe comfortably, you can see acceptably, and hear well.
- Is your costume suited for the temperature in which you plan to wear it? Will body odor be a problem? (Nothing worse than a hot stinky witch or a devil with perspiration lines).
- Is it designed to provide for enough mobility to allow you to enjoy yourself, or protect yourself against retaliating trick-or-treaters? Do you plan to run, dance, limbo, etc.?

☠ Is there the possibility of skin irritation or sensitivity from either makeup or costume? If so, go to work the next day as "Rash Monster".

☠ Do you plan to eat with this costume on?

☠ Will you be causing radio frequency interference to cell phones, radios, TVs, or computers?

☠ Can you use the bathroom…by yourself?

☠ Are you going to wear underwear under this thing, or at least wear something that would prevent you from being arrested if something happened to the costume, and you had to walk home without it.

☠ Could your costume be attracting other animals, insects, reptiles, or worse yet, children?

☠ Are you flame retardant, or just retardant?

☠ Are there any pockets to carry wallets, keys, or trick-or-treat candy?

☠ If borrowed, has anyone ever died in this costume, and if so, why?

Cost: Most of us live under this little umbrella called a budget. Factors affecting price include:

☠ To Buy or Rent the costume (Buy the cheap stuff, rent the fancy ones).

☠ Level of detail and realism (some of the illusion costumes can run between $500-$1200).

☠ Quality (will it last the night, or at least through the nacho dip).

☠ Where to shop to either buy it, or rent it, prices for the same items can vary significantly.

☠ If you buy it, hit the stores near or after Halloween for next year's costume, discounts range anywhere from 25% - 75%.

☠ Popularity, (Hillary Clinton costumes are big this year, especially in Africa and parts of Latin America, if you feel tough, try wearing a Barney® costume to a kids party).

Availability: Try to purchase early in the season for best selection. The season can start as early as late August. Review the listings of retailers, web sites, and catalogs in the last chapter, remember it's better to get the size a little large than too small. Makeup can be much more comfortable to wear for long periods compared to a latex mask. Of course, if you rent, also reserve it very early, like July / August.

Desired Effect: Just what kind of emotional reaction are you looking for this year, Elvira or Elvis, a monster or a monkey, a gory mad surgeon's victim or a box of popcorn, consider these possible moods:

- Sheer Terror - Frightful
- Humorous - Comical
- Sensuous - Sexy
- Theatrical - TV
- Mysterious
- Alien - Space Mystic
- Happy - Friendly
- Repulsive - Disgusting
- Amusing - Unusual - Creative
- Popular

Subject: This is the big question that most people get hung up on, "What should I be this year?"

- Some Type of Animal:
  - domestic or wild
  - bird or fish
  - reptile or mammal
  - house broken or free spirited
  - living or extinct
  - big or small
  - furry or smooth
  - realistic or animated

- A cartoon, comic strip, or comic book character (Popeye®, Charlie Brown®, Hagar®, Archie®, Dagwood®)
- Fairy Tail, Story Book or Mythological Figures:
  - Little Red Riding Hood
  - Goldilocks
  - a witch or wizard
  - a troll
  - a gnome
  - Paul Bunyon
  - Pecos Bill
  - Icabod Crane
  - Cinderella
  - a king or queen
  - Hercules
  - Mother Goose character
  - Wizard of Oz®
  - Pinocchio
  - Winnie Pooh Bear
  - Robin Hood
  - Medusa
  - Fairy Godmother
  - tooth fairy
  - a leprechaun
  - A giant
  - a knight
  - a prince
  - a jester
  - an executioner
  - a monk
  - a dragon
  - a warrior

- a lawyer that doesn't charge for advice

- A headhunter

☠ Some type of large bug or spider, flying or walking (dragonfly, ant, a bee, a firefly, a lady bug, a fly)

☠ Futuristic figures like aliens (use your imagination)

☠ Super Heroes and Villains:

- 💣 Batman®
- 💣 Robin®
- 💣 Superman®
- 💣 Wonder Woman®
- 💣 the Flash®
- 💣 the Penguin®
- 💣 The Riddler®
- 💣 Elastic Man®
- 💣 Cat Woman®
- 💣 Green Lantern®
- 💣 Power Rangers®

☠ Space Heroes:

- 💣 Star Trek®
- 💣 Star Wars®
- 💣 X-Files®
- 💣 Lost in Space®
- 💣 My Favorite Martian®

☠ A figure dressed from a past era (30s, 40s, 50s, 60s, 70s).

☠ A company mascot or logo (Mr. Clean®, Mr. Peanut®).

☠ A school mascot (cardinal, wildcat).

☠ A ghost, a skeleton, a zombie or a corpse, or even a big head or hand, devil, angel.

☠ A character from a famous sculpture or other piece of art.

☠ Mona Lisa, the Screamer, or other famous portrait figures.

☠ Illusion costumes:

These costumes are designed that make it look as though you are being held captive or being carried when in fact half your body is in the lower portion of the costume to walk around, and the upper portion is exposed in some unusual situation. The costume character's upper body is designed to look like the prop character is in control, and has you captive (see illustration). Variations for this costume could include:

- 💣 a corpse, a skeleton, a vampire, or a grave digger carrying you in a coffin
- 💣 a large man carrying you in a garbage can
- 💣 a hunter, a large wild animal, or a large bird carrying you in a cage
- 💣 a witch, or warlock, carrying you in a large black caldron
- 💣 you could be riding piggy-back on an old lady, an ape, or an explorer
- 💣 you could be resting in a chair or outhouse
- 💣 Remember that in each case, the legs that look like the figure's are really yours, the figure's upper body is part of the costume. The upper body of the figure being carried or captured is yours, but the legs are fake.

☠ Misc.:

- a time traveler
- a centaur
- a convict
- a hula dancer
- a mermaid
- an ameba

☠ Some type of food that you eat: Example: Clear Plastic garbage bag with colored balloons and labeled like a bag of jelly beans, try these:

- a pack of french fries
- a loaf of bread
- a hot dog or sandwich
- a type of candy bar, bag, or stick
- a can of soup
- a jar of peanut butter
- a pack of gum
- a doughnut or pickle
- a banana
- a bunch of grapes
- a milkshake
- a box of popcorn

☠ Some type of object:

- a TV
- a lighthouse
- a roll of toilet paper
- a grandfather clock
- a type of doll
- a toy, action figure
- a stuffed animal
- a refrigerator
- a working boom box
- a phone booth
- a fire hydrant
- a hot air balloon
- a mail box
- the sun or moon
- a vertical variable speed drill press
- a cigarette lighter
- a tornado funnel with little houses and things attached to the sides
- a computer w/monitor
- a car, bus, or truck
- a barber pole
- a packing box
- a lamp

☠ A celebrity:

- movie or TV star
- a singer
- an athlete
- a Ninja
- a politician
- A historical figure (Robin Hood, Ben Franklin)
- Tarzan®
- a children's show/movie
- Disney characters®, or even Barney®
- a race car driver
- Elvira®
- News caster
- The Crypt Keeper®
- Barbie® & Ken®

☠ A monster:
- traditional (Frankenstein® Wolfman®)
- current horror movie
- Pinhead®
- a mad, or muted person

☠ By profession:
- a pirate
- a magician (complete with a few parlor tricks)
- a police person (with squirt gun)
- a private detective (with Groucho Marx glasses)
- highly deformed nuclear energy employee
- a fortune teller
- a ballerina
- a fire fighter
- a bum
- a military person (Navy, Army, Marines, Air Force)
- an athlete
- auto mechanic
- a teacher
- construction worker

- crazed scientist
- Freddy Krueger®
- a Chain saw Killer
- a large animal or insect

- a cowboy or Native American
- an alien
- a doctor or Surgeon (with body parts in your pockets)
- an Optometrist (with thick funny glasses)
- a Dentist (with necklace of teeth or fake bad teeth)
- a computer geek
- a politician
- a hunter or fisher
- a nun, minister, rabbi or priest
- a clown
- photographer
- a gypsy
- a lawyer (if no one will recognize you)

- the Grim Reaper
- a killer clown
- one of the Munsters®
- One of the Addams Family®

- a maid or butler
- a chef or baker
- an engineer
- an accountant
- a butcher
- a plumber or repair person

- a painter
- an artist
- a carpenter
- a pilot
- a grave digger
- a mortician
- a New York cab driver
- A Blown up fireworks lighter

Other Considerations:

If you plan to be working in low lighting, your costume, mask, or makeup doesn't need to look as realistic. If you plan to be working under UV lighting (black lights), then you'll need to test the make-up ahead of time to see what shows up, and the effect it gives. Some eye drops even show up under UV, so test it ahead of time.

If you can make enough to buy a different one for next year, think about trading or selling a costume that turns out well after you've worn it. Try to buy closeout supplies after the holiday at huge discounts for the next year.

Realize if you get good at this, you can make all your kids' trick-or-treat costumes, and maybe even their school outfits, and save a ton of money.

Make-up:

As we mentioned earlier, we won't spend much time with makeup, since that can be the topic of an entire book by itself, but here are the basics. Most of the retailers and catalog companies carry a wide variety of makeup kits, and attachable accessories. When you purchase the kit for the type of figure you have decided to be, (or something close enough that you can make it adapt), all the needed accessories, glues, color greases, and instructions are provided. Like a no-brainer, dude.

When you can't find the right kit, or have several little goblins to dress up, keep these tips in mind. Theatrical make-up is your cheapest bet, and can be purchased at theatrical supply, costume, party, novelty, beauty supply, and magic stores year round. It can be found at drug, department, and toy stores near the holiday. You can either buy these supplies individually, or in sets. It will help you avoid overlooking something if you try to have some idea of the character you wish to make-up, and develop a specific list of supplies needed before visiting the make-up supply store.

A Summary of Tips To Follow When Applying Make-up:

- Clean oil and dirt from your face first with soap and water
- Apply or attach accessories that must be glued on first with the exception of hair or jewelry
- When adding skin parts always glue them in place before putting on the make-up to allow you to cover any color differences or glue marks and to improve adhesion.

- Use skin putty to build up for bumps, scars, warts, etc., or buy them already made of latex and stick them on. Body part extensions like noses, ears, warts, scars, gashes, chins, etc. are made of flexible latex to allow a natural look. There is a variety of flexible adhesives like rubber cement, spirit gum, etc. and can be used to pinch skin together for nice looking scars.

- Apply foundation coloring with the lightest colors first, layering the darker shades for shadowing and facial lines next
- Cover all exposed skin surfaces, including neck and hands with foundation coloring
- Use white or colored talcum powders to dull or mute colors or shiny reflections from grease paint
- Apply teeth, hair, jewelry, and fake blood last
- Check books out of the library, use encyclopedias, or surf the net

for color photos to model your make-up from

- Put make-up on sparingly, too much will cake up. Run together, smear and make a big mess
- Sometimes putting on a fine layer of Vaseline first allows for easier cleanup afterward, but not too much, or the makeup will easily smear, do not use if gluing on parts or using skin putty.

False teeth can add a lot when you buy the good kind. There are several dentists who sell joke sets that look great. Make sure if you wear teeth, you secure them with a safe oral adhesive or gum so they aren't always flapping around. If you decide to eat, do us all a favor, and remove those fake teeth.

Crepe hair and wigs won't fit right if they look really cheap, or wear a hat, bandanna, headband, or scarf over it. Try to come close to matching your eyebrow and nasal hair colors. You might want to add slight patches of hair growing out of warts, your nose, ears, or …oh, never mind.

Get creative with other accessories like:

- gluing a fly to your forehead
- a small worm coming out of an ear
- eye patches or fake eyes (half of a Ping-Pong ball painted)

- jewelry like nose rings and chains

- horns
- fake body piercing pins

- antenna
- Don't forget the finger nails

Rubber cement can be used to make very realistic looking …never mind again.

With a little practice, you'll look like you do this for a living, but only for Halloween. Remember, make-up is much more comfortable for long periods of time when compared to latex masks, or wearing a sheet as a ghost.

Support Props:

Support props are as important to the costume as frosting is to the cupcake. In most cases they can be very easy to fabricate at home, and can even add humor when they turn out a little disfigured. You can also buy about anything you need at the larger party and costume retailers. Unusual props can often be purchased in a related museum gift shop. Check the reference chapter for listings. Try to get props that you can attach to your costume so you don't have to tote it around the entire evening.

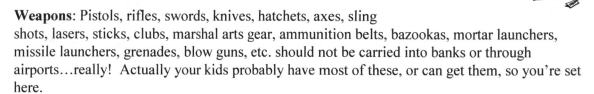

Clothing: Capes, cloaks, veils, scarves, gloves, hats, belts, holsters, boots, spurs, visors, goggles, helmets, etc. are sometimes more difficult to fabricate to look authentic, and may need to be rented, borrowed, or purchased.

Weapons: Pistols, rifles, swords, knives, hatchets, axes, sling shots, lasers, sticks, clubs, marshal arts gear, ammunition belts, bazookas, mortar launchers, missile launchers, grenades, blow guns, etc. should not be carried into banks or through airports…really! Actually your kids probably have most of these, or can get them, so you're set here.

Animals/Insects/Reptiles: Parrots, owls, bats, spiders, snakes, lizards, worms, alligators, cats, rats, ants, ticks, mice, termites, dust mites, etc. need to look realistic unless you're going for laughs. Whoever saw blue worms or green dust mites. If you ever find yourself bored on a rainy Saturday afternoon, call someone from the Audubon society, and ask if they can tell you where you can buy a half dozen stuffed owls, then get ready to duck.

Miscellaneous Props: Magic wands, bones, skulls, chains, shackles, crystal ball, pitch fork, rubber chicken, magic tricks (glowing thumb, disappearing coins, magic scarves), novelty jokes (shocking lighter, exploding pen, snapping gum), radios, beepers, cell phones, bird cage with hand puppet bird, ventriloquist dummy, lighted glasses, peg legs, hand hooks, portable toilets, coffins, etc.

Make it Yourself: Some of the most imaginative, frightful, and humorous costumes are home-made. Obviously we don't have the space to describe how to build each costume, so we will discuss two different ideas just to show you how easy it can be. The secret is in having a determined attitude that anything can be fabricated, a little imagination and creativity in selecting materials, a little design engineering in laying out a pattern or plan of construction, and a little patience in putting it together. Surprisingly, once you've made your first one and gained a little self-confidence, you tend to look forward to the annual challenge of what to make this year. Remember, when you custom design and fabricate your own costume, no one else will have it. I'll give you an example of how easy it can be:

EXAMPLES:

French Fries:

- ☠ Either find a cardboard box measuring approximately 36" wide x 18" x 40" high (to resemble a familiar large French fries carton, or construct one out of a larger cardboard box if needed by cutting open the sides and trimming to size, then taping corners closed.

- ☠ Cut out familiar crescent moon shapes of top front and back of box (buy a large fries to get container for model)

- ☠ Buy foam rubber sheets at either a fabric store or an Upholstery repair shop that measures about at least 18" in length and 2" – 3" thick, width can vary since you'll be cutting into 2" – 3" sections representing the thickness of each French Fry, but you'll need enough foam for about 30-35 fries.

- ☠ Use very sharp large scissors or razor blade knife to cut out French fries 3" x 3" x 18." Trim one end up to resemble the look of a French fries (see the ones you bought as a model if you haven't eaten them already).

- ☠ Buy four sheets of red poster board and one yellow, cut to cover each side of the box, and glue to the sides of the box (spray adhesive prevents rippling) to resemble the familiar red carton of a large order of fries.

- ☠ Very lightly in pencil trace out one of the two arches approximately 18" high on the dull side of the yellow poster board, when desired shape is achieved, cut it out and use it as a template to trace a second arch, then cut it out as well.

- ☠ Glue or paste (spray adhesive) the arches onto the front of the fries contained in centered in the middle of the box, or what ever is the current package design style.

- ☠ Cut two large holes in the bottom of the box for legs, cut arm holes in the sides.

- ☠ Make two fabric straps at least 2" wide, and about 20" long, out of a white fabric or strapping. Attach them to the inside walls of the box, each positioned about 12" from each end of the box, and about 4" from the top edge (see drawing). These straps are designed to hang over your shoulders (like suspenders) to hold the box up around you.

- ☠ Begin to hot glue the fries around the top inside edge of the box with the first row exposing between 8" – 12" of the fries over the top of the carton all the way around in the box. A second row behind these will be glued exposing 14" – 17" all around the inside of the box except in the middle of the front where your face sticks out. (put on box and test positioning of fries before hot gluing them on).

Wow! You're fries, now where's that ketchup when you need it? Pretty simple, and not too expensive.

The Garbage Man's Assistant:

- ☠ You'll need:
  - 💣 an old one-piece zipper fronted pair of overalls (not bib type)
  - 💣 one round 30 – 40 Gallon round plastic garbage can
  - 💣 a pair of old work gloves
  - 💣 an old pair of dress pants
  - 💣 an old pair of socks
  - 💣 an old pair of shoes
  - 💣 some foam stuffing or old rags
  - 💣 an old shirt
  - 💣 a full head latex mask for the garbage man
  - 💣 two 34" sections, two 12" sections, and one 10" section of 1.5"-2 " PVC pipe, (total of about 9')
  - 💣 two 90 degree PVC bend elbows
  - 💣 one PVC "T" section of matching pipe diameter
  - 💣 some pipe glue, and a hot glue gun.

- ☠ Sew or hot glue the socks onto the inside of the old dress pants legs of the pants to allow foam fill to be stuffed in for shape afterward at a height that would match the position if being worn by a man.

- ☠ Stuff the pant legs and socks with foam fill or rags to desired full shape.

- ☠ Hot glue the socked feet into the old shoes.

- ☠ Hot glue the pants onto the inside of the trash can so the legs are hanging out over the front of the trash can giving the natural appearance that a person is sitting inside the can with their legs out.

- ☠ Construct the PVC pipe so that you have a 34" section into an elbow with a 12" section, forming an "L". The other end of the 12" section fits into one end of the top of the T. Use the other 12" and 34" sections the form a second "L", and attach it to the opposite end of the "T" section, with the base of the T attached to the 10" section (see drawing).

- ☠ Hot glue the latex mask to the buttoned collar of the shirt, and stuff mask with foam until normal shaping is achieved.

- ☠ Take gloves and stuff with foam fill to natural shape, and hot glue each to the inside ends of the overall's sleeves.

- ☠ Hot glue gloves to bottom of the trashcan to give appearance that can is being held.

- ☠ Insert PVC pipe frame into arms of overalls so the T and 12" sections are across the shoulders with 10" section acting as a neck, slide ends of 34" sections down into the sleeves and into gloves then stuff arms with foam fill to a natural shape.

- ☠ Cut a hole along the side of the zipper from the base of the overalls up about 10" – 12" to allow the zipper to still function, but making a large enough hole to allow for you to slide your legs and lower body into the overalls with the top half of your body sticking outside the overalls in the trash can.

- ☠ Attach head to 10" section of PVC, then zip up overalls to the top around head in shirt, hot glue the shirt to the inside of the overalls.

- ☠ Tie one of the sections of cloth strapping in a secure knot around the middle of one of the 12" PVC sections, do the same with the other 12" section. Have the opposite ends of the fabric straps extending down and out of the hole left around the zipper of the overalls at the waist. These will be tied around your waist to snug the figure around you, giving the illusion that he is carrying you in the can.

- ☠ Stuff the arms and chest with foam fill around PVC pipe until the arms, chest, shoulders and neck of the Garbage Man figure look natural.

- ☠ Hot glue or sew a section of black fabric to the base of the chests, sealing in foam fill with top half of figure, but leaving out the tie down straps described in step 13 to tie costume in place.

- ☠ Cut out a section of the top half of the back of the trash can to allow your body to fit inside the can, but remember, since the can is being held at an angle you shouldn't cut the opening to the bottom of the can or it might destroy the illusion. Hold can up to overalls to help judge cutting.

- ☠ Also, hot glue or sew sections of black fabric to the insides of the opening cut in the trash can and inside opening of the overalls leaving enough room for you to slide your body in and out of the costume, while masking where your body comes out of the overalls. (see drawing)

- ☠ Now, slip your legs into the overalls, put on some work boots, tie the figure securely around your waist, and find a full-length mirror to see how things turned out!

PROPS TO ADD TO THE HORROR

This chapter walks you through the menagerie of
Halloween props. These are the trimmings you will find
that add so much to the general atmosphere of your
haunted experience. Each section provides an overview of
what is available in the stores or catalogs, approximate
price ranges, what you can do with them, along with ways
to make your own when it's reasonable. We cover a pretty
broad range of props, from a simple rat, bat, or jack-o-
lantern, to coffins, to devices for punishment. We even
expose you to professional animated props.

Some people find that by reading this chapter alone, they
can design their entire layout. Of course, these are the
same people who try to assemble their new 300-piece gas
grill without using the instructions. Remember to contact
us with any neat props you pick up, think up, whip up, spit
up, or stumble across that we don't already discuss in this
book.

BUILD OR BUY:

With this information you must choose
to either build or buy each prop needed.
The prop building can be a rewarding
group experience, and lead to personal
development of new skills, your choice
to build vs. buy will be best decided
when considering these situations:

- ☠ Do you have anyone working with
  you that is creative and artistic, or
  had experience with the mediums
  you intend to use (wood working,
  metals, sculpting, painting)? Are
  they willing to work for the fun of
  it???
- ☠ Is the lighting going to be
  minimized, so you can use
  homemade props with poor detail
  in the shadows?
- ☠ Do you have the time and place to
  construct them? Things can get
  messy.

- Though in many cases the supplies are easily found at a building supply, hardware, upholstery, or fabric stores, certain skills and tools are often required. Ask yourself, if it is cost effective when buying specialty items that must ordered in large quantities for the number you need?

- For fundraising haunted attractions - Have you already exhausted efforts to get commercial donations for the funding of prop purchases, or asked vendors for prop donations, or even to borrow them?

- Have you checked to see if any local universities or high school art departments would be willing to help with the construction project of a fundraiser?

STORING YOUR PROPS:

Regardless of whether you construct or purchase your props, you will quickly amass a significant investment in them. You will also have to store them somewhere. Keep that in mind when you develop your plan on how and where you plan to get your props. The ideal situation to use household items whenever possible. This way you can return the items to their normal use afterwards. Also, borrow whenever possible. Borrow from friends, stores relatives, etc., but never from cemeteries, unless you don't mind having unsolicited visitors late at night seeking their return. Ask your garbage man and junk dealer to keep an eye out.

Instead of storing larger props, use them for something else during the off season. For example, a coffin makes a real conversation piece of a coffee table. Particularly when you use a glass top and leave either the skeleton or corpse inside. Have the skeleton holding a doll or teddy bear for a warmer homey effect.

To help extend the useful life of these props, try to follow these simple storage guidelines:

- Always avoid storage areas that experience extreme temperatures, heat or cold. Nothin' worse than cooked corpse!

- Store props in a dry space to avoid mold (though maybe a little might look good).

- Keep anything made from latex in plastic bags to prevent drying or discoloration.

- Store small and medium sized props in boxes, and protect them by wrapping in packing paper, newsprint, or bubble wrap. Never wrap lightly colored props in newspaper due to possible ink staining, use butcher paper, blank news print, or packing paper.

- ☠ Keep hollow latex items, like masks, stuffed with paper to maintain their shape.

- ☠ Remove all batteries before storing electronic props.

- ☠ Wrap all glass in bubble wrap (available at office supply and moving supply stores).

- ☠ Store liquids topside up and sealed in plastic bags in case of leakage.

- ☠ Keep coffin lids closed to avoid dust, and midnight escapes.

- ☠ Never ever store jack-o-lanterns carved out of real pumpkins, unless you choose to freeze them.

- ☠ Avoid storage of life-sized skeletons, corpses, or costumed mannequins, and dummies in dark isolated areas, like under the house. The bug exterminator, building inspectors, plumbers, or electricians may stumble across them. You wouldn't believe what these people might do to your home to retaliate.

- ☠ Unplug all electric chairs when left unattended.

BODY PROPS:

A body prop can be made out of a wide variety of household items, **including** your spouse or in-laws. We try to discuss several options here, so that you can utilize the raw materials that are most available to you. The ideal corpse would be made primarily out of latex, and that can get expensive. We'll include all types of life sized figures in this section including skeletons, dummies, mannequins, and inflatables…on second thought, maybe we'll just skip the inflatables.

SKELETONS are one of your most effective props (particularly when they are of humans), but real ones can be the most difficult to find. Real skeletons can be ordered from select medical supply houses (check with a local university's School of Medicine), with prices starting at over $700, and can go as high as several thousand dollars for certain specimens. Occasionally, you can find one at a flea market, but even there it will probably cost at least $300. There may be state laws restricting ownership of human remains so either check first, or be prepared to tell curious onlookers, "Are you kidding, where do you think someone could get a REAL skeleton?" The author had one for 24 years, but was pressured by his better half to get rid of it, something about not having dead bodies around.

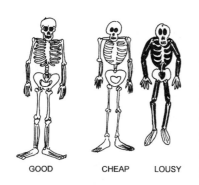

GOOD   CHEAP   LOUSY

We list several companies that deal in anatomical supplies and sell ARTIFICIAL life-sized wired skeletons, skulls, etc. They usually start at about $200 for a really cheap one, and go up to about $1500. The Brainstorm catalog, listed in the last chapter, has a real good one for only $300. On a rare occasion, you might find a bargain at a university medical department or high school science department getting rid of an old model that needs repairs, and is missing some bones.

Inexpensive skeleton props sold at Halloween supply stores usually look about as real as that chest toupee with the gold chain you use to wear to the bars during your college days. So, make sure if that's your choice, keep the lights down low.

A final note, always contact the authorities first whenever you stumble across a real skeleton. It's like finding money, they have to hold it for a while to see if someone claims it before they can give it to you. Besides, it may just lead to trouble. Whoever saw a fake skeleton haunt a house?

A CORPSE is the prop most people are "dying" to get their hands on. They really aren't too difficult to construct, and can be a great addition to any haunted house. There is a book listed in the reference chapter that provides a highly detailed step-by-step set of instructions to construct a corpse that looks so good, any forensic lab would be proud to display it. These things have lighted eyes, can be built with moveable jaws, and have teeth that would make that weight challenged female Russian wrestler that worked in your high school cafeteria jealous. The beauty about these plans is that almost everything you'll need is easily available. Once you see what these things look like, it doesn't take much imagination to come up with a hundred ways to have fun with a corpse well after Halloween.

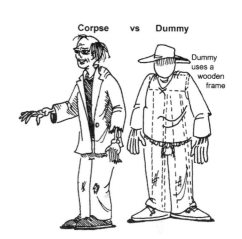

Corpse vs Dummy

Dummy uses a wooden frame

To buy a corpse can be quite expensive. They can start at about $175, and quickly climb up to $500 - $1,000. You can get a real nice one for around $500. We can hear you from here, "500 bucks, is that guy nuts?" By the time you finish this book, you'll have your answer there, but that's why we included a section on how to build your own corpse. Obviously, if you invest significant dollars on a top-notch corpse, it should be used in a highly visible scene, or with a drop and scare trick, to get your money's worth. You could save a lot of money if you have a friend into taxidermy, and know someone that has really been bugging you lately...never mind.

Regardless of where you find your corpses, they are a key ingredient to any first class Halloween layout, and can reduce your need for live volunteers in costume. Particularly in cases where it's difficult to find volunteers to go into that musty old coffin, or get dropped through the ceiling with a noose around their neck. Check the reference chapter for specific corpse vendors.

DUMMIES are by far the most routinely used prop in Halloween displays. They can be easily constructed with a night-visit into Dad's closet, and look great in limited light situations. They even sell dummies now for around $100 that can be used to ride with you in your car for security, but most use them for driving in the HOV lanes at rush hour.

Dummies look best when created with a life-like head by using a latex mask and wig. Some interesting derivations have been heads fabricated using a nylon stocking, some fiber fill, and some dark thread. Another entertaining option is to build in your dummy with an animated head (like a ventriloquist dummy) which can be manipulated by a hidden assistant. Also consider hiding a speaker or tape player inside your dummy for an additional scare.

MANNEQUINS are ideal to dress up in costume for any haunted layout. They can be expensive when buying one in good or new condition, with some designer models selling for a few thousand dollars. We recommend looking for old, out of style and damaged models. You should even look for ones missing limbs. You can often find spare parts or just leave the sucker maimed. Second hand business equipment stores, or classified listings under business equipment and supplies are good leads. See if they have anything they would donate to enjoy the tax write-off, or maybe you can borrow a few.

Mannequins are handy, because unlike most dummies, they have a ridged frame that can be stood upright, and can usually be posed. The older ones have very realistic-looking glass eyes. Surprisingly, it's quite a challenge dressing these things, so you might want to practice first on your spouse next time they fall sound asleep on the living room sofa. Oh yes, a suggestion to the husbands out there. Inform your spouse before attempting to dress a female mannequin in the garage or basement. This can prevent an embarrassing, and potentially discrediting, situation when caught by surprise.

USING A HEAD PROP: The head prop differs from using a mask due to its ability to be free standing. It also has eyes and usually better detail. Most sold are made of latex, but one can be made using a Styrofoam wig stand and various accessories to be glued on for detail of eyes, teeth etc. Use paint, makers, Ping-Pong balls, or whatever else is available. See the next page for steps to build a latex head prop.

BUILD YOUR OWN CORPSE OR DUMMY:

While describing the steps and options necessary for the construction of your corpse, we segment our discussion into the head, hands and feet, and body. We feel obligated to mention that grave robbing is a crime in all states.

Your first step is to locate the outfit this corpse is going to be laid to rest in. Male or female, most people are buried in more formal attire. This includes dark colored suites, dresses, etc. Accident victims are another story. Just make up your mind, so you can begin construction. You must select the outfit first, because we're going to custom build the corpse to fit the clothes, like they build a coffin to fit the body.

A quick note before moving ahead. Go to second hand shops, flea markets, garage sales, church bazaars, accident scenes, mortuaries, or your relatives clothes closet on the next family visit to obtain the outfit for your "body-to-be." You can even borrow your buddy's driver's license for ID, and go to a formal wear rental shop. You probably have something tucked in the back of your own closet that you could use that is if you want this layout to be a comedy.

Jerry Chavez, author of , "Haunted House Halloween Handbook" had a web page at http://members.aol.com/spookyfx/index.html in which he describes how to build a corpse out of a cheap $10 plastic life-size skeleton, and supplies that are inexpensive and easy to find. Write me if you can't find it. Oh yes, if anyone asks what you're reading, you can inform them that you're reading a book on "Body Building"!

HEADS:

Your choices here are to buy a prop head, build a prop head as described on the previous page, or use a mask to fabricate a head.

MAKING A HEAD:

To buy a prop head visit our resource chapter and review vendor web sites and catalogs. To build a prop head takes a little time, and can become expensive when building just one due to the expense of the materials in small quantities. The advantages of building vs. buying include developing the skills to build and design unique props unavailable at stores. This will significantly add to the effect and realism of your haunt once you improve your talents to produce authentic looking props. Our discussion will center on the use of latex, since it is pliable, lightweight, and looks the most realistic. Realize that once you develop these skills you will almost be qualified to perform plastic surgery.

Here's what to do:

1) You need to find a base to use to mold the latex around. Your best choices are either a Styrofoam wig stand, or build a life-sized plastic model of a human head or skull. You could even make a good paper-mache life-sized model of a head, though this does require more artistic skills, and prior experience.

2) If you plan to add eyeballs or teeth, glue these in before applying latex, so you can model around them to cover gaps, and make it look more realistic. Eyes and teeth can be purchased at any Halloween prop, Novelty, or Magic & Joke store. Glass eyeballs cost about $20-$30 each, but look great. Teeth can be bought from vendors listed in the resource chapter and through web site browsing. Bucky Teeth© look realistic and come in a variety of styles. Also, check in that glass on the nightstand next to grandma's bed. You could even make eyeballs and teeth for those who are creatively artistic. Eyeballs can be painted on Ping-Pong ball halves.

3) If you are using a wig stand or a model without the seven standard head orifices, you may want to either carve them or drill them out (nose, ears, eye sockets and mouth). Nothing more humiliating than to have some kid notice that your corpse is without orifices.

4) The next step is to purchase about a quart can of liquid latex from an art supply store, then start painting on the first layer of latex over the head. If you want to build up areas that aren't already part of your foundation model, use nose putty, body putty, etc. before applying the latex. This might include noses, ears, lips, or areas around and under the chin when using a skull model. You can also buy these facial accessories, and glue them on with rubber cement, shoe glue, or other rubber adhesive.

5) Once the first coat of latex has dried, begin painting on a second coat. Add little pieces of cotton, clay, or shredded paper-mache in with the second third and fourth layers of latex to add a decaying texture. To mix paper mache; add 1 cup of flour to 1 - 1.5 cups of water (depending on desired texture), 1-2 teaspoons of salt, and optional 1-4 tablespoons of carpenter's wood glue for additional durability.

6) Continue to add coats by painting on liquid latex mixture until the desired look is achieved. Avoid applying applications too thickly, resulting in the loss of definition and detail, and for heaven sakes, don't over paint and block your orifices. A nice effect is to build up veins with nose putty that will later be painted a dark blue. Also, build several large ugly moles too.

7) Once the final coat of latex has dried (allow about three days), begin to apply latex paint (available at an art supply store, but be sure to tell the store clerk for what you plan to use the paint). Begin painting with the lightest tone base color. Depending on the desired degree of decay, the lighter the color, the fresher the corpse. Colors might start with a white or pale yellow/green and work through the spectrum to a dark brown. Be sure to mix a little extra of the base color so you don't run out when you paint the hands, or to paint over the glue line if you apply any hair. If you don't find latex paint, mix acrylic paint with the liquid latex, and paint that on. The ratio is four parts latex to one part paint.

8) After painting the base color, darken it, and paint shadows around eyes and where there are deep facial lines. When painting a more decayed state skin in a darker color, no darker shades are needed.

9) Next, paint the lips and any veins a dark blue, then paint eyes and any teeth an off white or pale yellow. Finally paint totally shadowed areas like inside mouth, nose holes, ear holes, etc. black, also finish painting any other areas not yet mentioned. Allow each color to dry first before painting the next.

10) If you decide to add some hair, buy crepe hair at a theatrical supply store, cut it to desired length, and glue one row at a time, in layers, starting at the base of the head, working upward in rows across the head.

Once the glue is dried, paint the glue line with the base paint used on the face, move up about a half inch and start the next row of hair. Continue until you have laid the desired amount of hair. This takes patience since each row must dry before moving to the next. When completed, comb out excess hair.

HAPPY BIRTHDAY, YOUR FIRST HEAD.

Get creative with the accessories that can be attached to the head. Look around at garage sales and second hand shops. Model the face to look just like a neighbor for additional laughs.

USING A MASK TO MAKE A HEAD:

The use of a full head latex mask to make a head offers more realism than to build up a wig stand.

- ☠ To maintain a natural shape, stuff it evenly with foam fiberfill, shipping Styrofoam chips, tightly packed newsprint paper, or for best results place the mask over a Styrofoam wig stand.

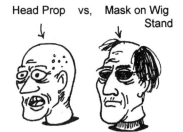

Head Prop   vs,   Mask on Wig Stand

- ☠ Hot glue black cloth or heavy plastic sheeting around the inside base of the neck to keep filler inside the head.

- ☠ Cut a small hole that will be used to insert a dowel rod through to attach the head to the body. The rod should allow about 8" inside the mask, and 10" outside to attach to body

- ☠ We recommend that you avoid cheap masks cast with thin latex, since it is difficult to maintain normal shape, and they don't look life-like.

No eye or mouth holes on head

- ☠ We do recommend that for the most frightening effect, use something that looks realistic, and not one of the "Space Clowns from Hell®" masks.

ATTACHING THE HEAD:

Once you've got the head, you need to insert a rod into the base of the head used for attachment to the body. Use either 1" or 2" wooden dowel rod, plastic conduit pipe, or similar PVC pipe. This may need to be glued in with Shoe Glue, epoxy glue, hot glue gun, etc. for increased stability. If you do this, you can't use the head independently as a prop. Leave at least 8"-10" extra rod out of the base of the neck to be used for attachment to the body.

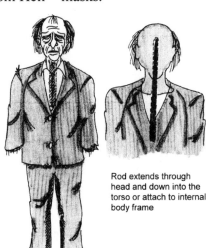

Rod extends through head and down into the torso or attach to internal body frame

HANDS:

MAKE YOUR OWN HANDS

As with the head, you have several choices here. The most common choice is to use a pair of gloves. Any kind work, dark or white looks best. Stuff each glove with cloth, paper, or foam fill to maintain shape. Gloves are hot glued or sewn to the inside surfaces of the sleeves of the clothes used for the figure.

Another technique is to add the ability to bend and position the fingers. To do this:

- ☠ Simply cut straight sections of heavy wire coat hanger to lengths of about 10" and twist the five sections needed per hand (one per finger and thumb) at one end, down about 3" from one end, so to give the appearance of a yard rake.

- ☠ Now, hold up one of the gloves that you plan to use. Lay the wire frame on top of it with the twisted ends facing the sleeve. Bend and then trim each piece of wire to match the shape and length of a finger and thumb of the glove.

☠ When this is done, take half inch thick sheets of foam rubber that can be purchased at any fabric store, and cut a strip 3"-4" wide. To cut strip to the proper length, hold the foam strip up to the wire finger frame finger trip and measure down to where the wires wrap together in the palm, and cut to length. Experimenting with one finger to establish necessary dimensions needed to give fingers a natural look.

☠ Now, wrap the foam snugly around the wire, and then, using either duct tape or cheap electrical tape, tightly wrap the foam in tape until achieving desired size and shape to match a normal finger or thumb.

☠ Once you decide the amount of foam needed to form a natural finger and thumb width, cut remaining pieces of foam. Use only two to three total wraps of tape around the foam to avoid wasting tape. Perform the same procedure to each remaining finger and thumb. Again, cut enough foam so fingers aren't too thin, and you're forced to compensate with excessive amounts of tape.

☠ Slide the glove over each hand, and lay aside for now to await attachment to arm.

LATEX GLOVE HANDS:

A final approach involves the use of latex gloves (the variety you can buy as cleaning gloves, not those worn by doctors). Again, follow the steps described above. Slide the foam wrapped wire frame into the glove, and paint to match head. For an added touch, buy a set of fake fingernails from a Halloween prop, costume, theatrical supplies, or any other store selling beauty or Halloween supplies. Securely glue these on with spirit gum or any glue that works well with rubber. Paint the hands with the same latex paint used for the head, paint the nails a dark blue. Use a black permanent marker to draw wrinkles on the fingers.

BUY COSTUME HANDS:

Another technique is to follow all the steps just listed, but instead of a pair of gloves, use a pair of latex costume hands, the thicker the latex the better. There are a wide assortment of style and colors, but try to find some that look like corpse hands. They range $5-$65. These can then be painted to match the head with the latex paint used when painting the head. Stuff for shape, and glue cloth or plastic over the ends to retain stuffing.

BUY PROP HANDS:

A third approach is to buy prop latex hands ($10-$20 each). You can simply cut sections of coat wire to length, and insert each down to the fingertips from the end of the wrist to provide for fingers to be posed. If the prop's hands aren't foam filled, add foam fiberfill or newsprint in from the wrist, until natural shape is achieved. These too can be painted with the latex paint to match the facial color. You can also buy head and hands together that match. When buying prop hands individually, check to see that you can get both a left and right hands. Also, skeleton hands are available, and give a creepy look, just be sure to get both left and right.

FEET

MAKE FEET USING SOCKS OR HOSE:

Use socks or hose stuffed with foam rubber fiber fill, packed tightly, and formed to a natural shape all the way up past the ankle by about 2"-3." Insert a 1"-2" diameter dowel rod cut to about 10." One end rests in the heal, and the other end sticks out of the neck of the sock to attach to the leg. Secure the ankle opening of the sock around the rod using a rubber band, and then seal sock around dowel rod with a hot glue gun to keep the foam filler inside. The sock can then be hot glued into a shoe or boot, or left like some "Flake" at the mortuary just forgot to put the shoes on. It's hard to find reliable help these days.

PURCHASE LATEX FEET:

Another approach is to purchase latex prop feet for a more realistic look. This will add to the costs ($10-$70 each), and once again, be sure to buy or order left and right feet. There are a variety phony feet to choose from, some attached to the calve of the leg, some gory. You can also paint these the color of the hands and face, but don't forget to paint those nasty nails black. Don't use socks or shoes when you go to the expense and effort to provide the detail of real feet.

BUY SKELETON FEET:

A final option is to buy skeleton feet. Again, be sure to get opposing feet or you may find this corpse constantly walking in circles.

Realize that sometimes you can avoid the feet and hands altogether. This is particularly true when building a corpse wearing an old suit. The sleeves and cuffs are tattered, and give the appearance that the hands and feet simply fell off. Scare Factory builds a prop called the Corpselator®, which includes a corpse in a coffin (without hands or feet) that jumps out about 6' on an actuator.

THE BODY:

BUILDING THE BODY:

When fabricating the body, once again, there are many options. The main component will be a frame built to support the head, hands, and feet. This frame can be built out of a variety of materials, but for our example we suggest using a 2"x4" board for the torso, and PVC pipe for the arms and legs. We recommend that you read through these simple step-by-step instructions once completely, then again to make your list of supplies to buy. You may decide to use another technique to construct a certain component based on available supplies at your local hardware or building supplies store. There are countless alternatives, so be creative and practical, but frugal.

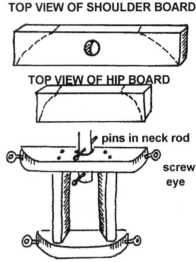

TOP VIEW OF SHOULDER BOARD

TOP VIEW OF HIP BOARD

pins in neck rod

screw eye

TORSO FRAME DESIGN

The frame will consist of one piece of wood for the shoulders, two pieces connecting the pelvis or hip board, and one piece for the pelvis. The arms and legs will be made of jointed 1.5" PVC pipe (2" PVC pipe for the thigh or femur bone).

- ☠ The first step is to measure the clothes that will be used to dress this thing. For the shoulder cross board, cut a 2"x4"section between 15"-20," depending on the size clothes you plan to dress the corpse in. To get specific measurement, lay shirt or blouse you plan to use down onto a table, and measure from left shoulder tip to the right shoulder tip, then subtract 2" for joints.

- ☠ The board will have the corners trimmed to narrow at the shoulder tips for a more natural look. Also, a hole the size of the neck rod used to support the head must be drilled in the center of the board (see illustration).

- ☠ For the Hip cross board, measure across the hips of the pants, and subtract only 1." This measurement will probably be between 10" - 16" (remember there is no such thing as a fat butt corpse). As with the shoulder board, the hip board will also have corners trimmed. Sideboards are optional, but can help improve shape. (See drawing).

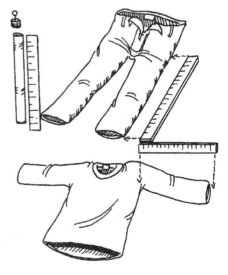

- ☠ Two boards will be used to connect the shoulder board and the hip board. Again, to determine this length, lay the clothes down on a table, and measure from the shoulders down to the hips (18" - 26"). Nail the two body boards between the shoulder and hip boards.

- ☠ The ends of the shoulder board and hip board will have 1" screw eyes inserted to provide for the arms and legs connections.

99

☠ It's optional how you decide to add bulk to the body, or if you even need to. We suggest that you finish the arms and legs, connect them, dress the frame, and then decide if the chest cavity needs more shape. If you decide it does, you can use several different materials. One option is to use a heavy duty black plastic trash bag filled with enough Styrofoam shipping chips, foam rubber fiber fill, newsprint, etc. until desired shape is achieved. Use duct tape to attach bags to wooden frame.

☠ Another option is to use a screening or wire mesh or chicken wire, all available at a building supplies store. Wrap and shape around the wooden frame.

☠ Another method is to use one half to one-inch foam rubber sheets that can be purchased at a fabric store. Simply cut sections and wrap it around frame sections until desired shape is achieved. Fasten with duct tape, staple gun, or hot glue gun. You can also use thicker sections of foam rubber cut to specific shape and hot glued into position. Buy this at a furniture upholstery store.

☠ A final method is to build up the chest by taping layers of rags or newsprint using duct tape to the wooden frame. The objective is to keep materials lightweight and cheap. It would be a shame for this thing to be hanging somewhere in the house, and then have it fall, crashing down one of your patrons.

ARMS AND LEGS:

☠ Again you have many materials and techniques to use here, but we feel the famous old PVC method is the way to go. It's light and cheap. Working with it may even lead you to a new career as a plumber. Use a hacksaw to cut it.

☠ You must cut the arms and legs sections to size. Measure the sleeve of the clothes to be used. Each arm will have two measurements, from the shoulder to the elbow, and from the elbow to the end of the sleeve. Then subtract 1." This should range between 8"-14" sections and the two measurements will be within 1" of each other. Copy these cuts for the opposite arm, unless this guy is supposed to look lopsided.

☠ Make the measurements for the legs, hip to knee, knee to ankle or end of the pant leg, and copy for the other leg. For dresses, measure your leg, then make adjustments for any size differences between your size and the clothes being used. No, this is not an invitation to test cross-dressing guys.

☠ Buy enough PVC to cut into the eight sections of desired lengths. Use 1.5" PVC pipe for the six sections used for both sections of the arms and lower legs. Use two sections of 2" PVC pipe for the thighs. For dummies with more bulk, either wrap these pipes in foam rubber sheeting until desired thickness is achieved, or buy larger diameter pipe. For simple dummies, just stuff a one-piece jump suit for the body, and attach stuffed gloves and socks with hot glue gun or sew on.

☠ Either buy matching diameter PVC end caps, or buy dowel rod to match the inside diameter of the PVC pipe sections, also buy PVC glue. These end caps will support the screw eyes used to make the attachments.

☠ You can even cut round pieces of wood that fit tightly into the ends of the PVC. You can also drill two small 1/4 inch holes through the sides of the PVC pipe about 3/8-1/2 inch from end of the pipe sections, and use heavy leather lacing with the section knotted on each end pulled through the pipe. If you use this approach, be sure to insert the lacing tightly through the pipe.

☠ The next step is to insert 1" screw eyes into the end caps or wood inserts of each section of PVC. The screw eyes will not be centered, but offset toward the inside to allow for improved bending of limbs toward the body. (see drawing) Tie leather lacing (use a double granny knot, or if you're an x-scout, do your own thing) to join the PVC sections to each other and to the body. There are a variety of hardware pieces that can be used to also connect the screw eyes, but when tied properly, the leather lacing provides improved movement, and can be easily repaired if broken.

☠ Now it's time to dress our little bambino for the funeral party, so put on shirt, pants, coats, tie, dresses, etc., underwear is not required, unless of course you're just that kind of person. We wonder if they actually bury people with underwear?

☠ If your corpse is a lady in a dress, use panty hose over the PVC pipes for the legs, and paint 4-6 layers of latex the color of the face and hands over the surface. You can also attach cotton wadding while applying latex for skin texture.

☠ Finally, attach the hands and feet the same way you attached the arms and legs, with leather shoe lacing through the screw eyes. If needed, make any final cosmetic adjustments by adding any extra clothing, foam, dirt or tears on clothing, hats, glasses, worms, etc.

☠ Now, to test how good it turned out, set it up in some dark corner, closet, bathroom, or where ever your spouse or friend might stumble across it. Oh yes, you'll also need a spare pillow and blanket to sleep out in the garage tonight.

HEADS USED AS A PROP:

It's suggested that if your audience includes small children, or sensitive adults, you consider skulls and skeleton hands as an alternative to severed body parts.

About 5-8 years ago it was difficult to find a realistic looking severed head without paying "an arm and a leg" for it, but now they're all over the place. These works of cultural art are priced from around $20 up to $100. Most are made of latex, but there are a few made of polyfoam, polyurethane, and polystyrene. Be aware that the harder materials may chip or dent easily. Options to consider when choosing your head to be used as a prop include:

- coloring
- level of gore, blood, and those nasty meaty detachment ends
- facial expression
- detail of casting and painting, use of hair

- realism
- materials used (thickness of latex, density of polyfoam fill)
- accessories (hair, jewelry, glass eyeballs, teeth, weapons, worms)

The most startling effects come from surprising visitors by exposing the head in an unexpected place with a sudden bust of light, and a loud scream sound effect. Suspending the head with non-reflective fishing line or black thread, or by positioning a black rod directly behind it into a wall gives that floating 3D effect. Add to the shock with the surprise of a sudden burst of air from a compressor air gun, and your talking "wet socks" here. If you want to get high-tech, have glowing eyes, movable jaw that can be operated by an unseen assistant, or rotating eyes by using components from an inexpensive remote control car's turning mechanism inside the head.

OTHER BODY PARTS:

By now you have probably seen enough of these things for yourself to realize that they have almost every body part you can imagine. Some come blood covered and gory looking, while others are just as they would look unattached. One company has parts in lab tanks that can even come with optional lighting and bubble kits. These tanks come with a skeleton hand, a severed hand, a face, a heart, and a brain. You could get creative on this and visit your local pet store, or stop by the butcher to browse today's 'leftovers."

Also, when attaching hands and arms to a wall consider using the screw-in garage hooks. Insert the hook into the hand through the severed end of the wrist, and screw the opposite end into the wall.

BUGS AND ANIMALS:

This section has been a favorite for the many years, because of their availability, and how they are often used as a practical joke that can be played year round. We guess hiding a disfigured human hand under a couch cushion doesn't evoke the same reaction, as would a rubber spider. We're sure that you've seen the small stuff out there, but the medium and larger sizes, realism, and materials distinguish the amateur from professional prop in this category. In select cases there are even the options of lights, sound and animation. Just plan to spend a lot more for these. Rubber bug and animal props have seen terrific growth in the past 5 years.

A great effect is to paint dark colored bugs with fluorescent paint, hang them from the ceiling in a dark room or closet using black thread. Have a hidden floor switch or helper on a switch, turn on a UV light positioned out of view of the audience at just the right moment. Use luminous paint on the bugs, then hit them with a short burst of very bright light. You could also use a closet or room with a door that can be closed, a helper turns on a bright light, then turns it off, and then the door reopens to expose a darkened room haunted by bug spirits.

MAKE YOUR OWN:

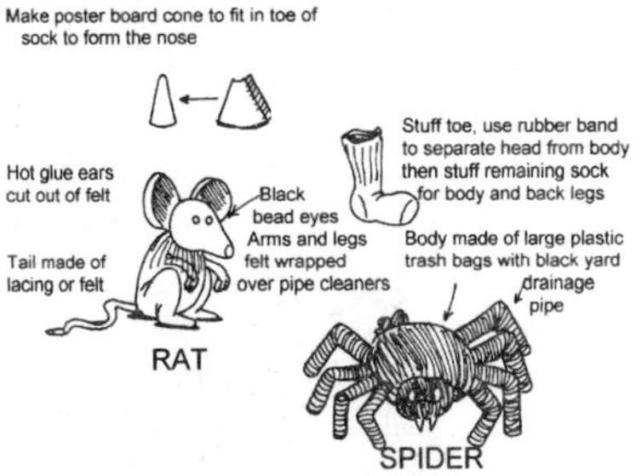

If you decide to make your own props, we suggest that you plan to use them under very low lighting or a strobe. It's difficult to build bug or animal props to look life-like in natural lighting, but your objective when making a prop like this should be for size and shape.

Make poster board cone to fit in toe of sock to form the nose

Hot glue ears cut out of felt

Tail made of lacing or felt

Black bead eyes

Arms and legs felt wrapped over pipe cleaners

RAT

Stuff toe, use rubber band to separate head from body then stuff remaining sock for body and back legs

Body made of large plastic trash bags with black yard drainage pipe

SPIDER

The materials recommended to construct a giant spider would include 8 sections of black bendable material like plastic conduit, drainage pipe, etc. for the legs, a large heavy duty black plastic trash bag stuffed with newspaper for the body, and a smaller stuffed black bag for the head. Use split fluorescent orange Ping-Pong balls for eyes. Form an impression in the bag for a mouth. Make teeth cut out of a section of either white or yellow poster board bent into the curvature of the mouth. Use synthetic fur glued around the outside of the head for an added effect (available at a fabric store).

Other ideas include using old stuffed black socks, sculpting shapes from blocks of foam rubber, and creating surface textures or skins with items available at fabric or upholstery stores. Just walking through a building supply store with a friend, and taking a short list of what you plan to make, will expose you to a variety of great materials that you and a hot glue gun can concoct into something better left under the porch. Fabric stores, craft stores, and costume supply stores will also provide a lot of useable materials.

BUYING YOUR PROPS:

When buying, use the list in our reference section, but also consider nature stores, large sporting goods stores, museum gift shops, and taxidermist's yard sales. If you find a wholesaler that is

closing out latex bugs, snakes, and spiders, consider buying enough to cover a floor that people must walk on (especially if the guests are without shoes).

On Bob's Halloween Page, a web site at http://srv02.anaserve.com/~bobandrews/lindey.html there were plans to construct an animated owl with remote controlled head and eyes (Using a decoy owl, cutting it open, and installing toy remote control car parts. Consider positioning what ever you use near a small speaker, using sound effects for added fun.

The fun thing about using bugs is that people expect to see them just about everywhere, but still hate to find them.

EVERYTHING ELSE SPOOKY AND CREEPY

As you could imagine, we could write a book alone on this category, so we'll only list a good representation. Be aware that about anything you would want, a device of punishment or torture, something from an evil lab, or something from the annals of an old haunted house, can probably be bought from somewhere. The majority can also be fabricated, and usually are.

COFFINS:

☠ These can be built out of either cardboard, fiberboard, wood, or even thick Styrofoam, or buy them used.

☠ If purchased, they may cost anywhere from $35 (cardboard)-$5,000 (metal, the real thing)

☠ Never buy a used coffin with a moon shaped hole cut into the top of the lid.

☠ For a large 8" tall design use 3 sheets of plywood board measuring 4'x8'x1" . Start with the board that will produce the sides of the coffin. Rip saw the board into 3 sections each 18" x 96". Cut D and E to 78", C and F to 24", A to 18" and B to 12" long. Now build the side frame first, then set it on top of each the two remaining boards to trace out the top and bottom of the coffin. Saw off the four corners on both boards. Both glue and nail the back board onto the side frame (unless building a trick coffin with rear entry). For the front or top attach 3 heavy duty hinges to the inside seam of one of the 78" long sides. Space hinges 6" from each end and the third in the center. Lid should open outward with hinges inside the coffin. Now attach the 4 handles to the outside frame of the coffin, 2 on the 24" sides, and 2 on the oposite ends of the 78 in sides Paint flat black, line with red satin. For smaller sizes trace

Sides of Coffin (16")	Top of Coffin	Bottom of Coffin

lines then cut lid and back first, then build the side frame to fit again using three 18" x 96" sections to build the frame from.

☠ If cutting out of cardboard, use duct tape on interior joints. Paint flat black., and add hardware handles made from pieces of rope knotted from the inside of the coffin.

TOMBSTONES:

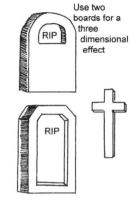

Use two boards for a three dimensional effect

☠ These are easy to construct of either Styrofoam, wood, cardboard, or particle board

☠ Epitaphs can be painted onto the tombstone directly, or printed onto paper then attached. When bought they cost $5-$50. Have fun with the epitaphs and see how many you can get that rhyme and are funny, or surf the net using the key word "epitaphs." If you have a router you can have a great effect on wood, or use a soldering iron for Styrofoam.

&* In this plot lies big fat Fred, too many pizzas, and now he's dead

&* Big and tough, t'was king of the mound, but now ol' Jake lies in the ground

&* A fancy eater was Diamond Phil, 'til the day he couldn't pay his bill

&* Quick on the draw Wild Pete was fast, until the day his bullet went on past

&* He beat his kids then punched his wife, but that mistake cost Jack his life

&* Ol' Joe played tricks on all he met, 'til he tried giving his wife a snake for a pet

TABLES:

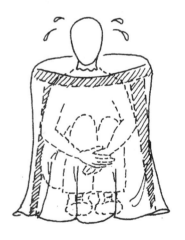

These tables could be used as an operating table, a torture table, or a table to support something, like a coffin. Your best bet is to try to buy an old used inexpensive four legged, rectangular wooden table with significant wear. You want it to be at least 48"x60," but if you can get one longer try for at least 72" to support the coffin.

If you plan to use it as an operating table (with partially hidden staff member allowing for illusions using body props), holes will need to be cut into the tabletop. The hole size and position rely on which parts of the body will be exposed, and which will be hidden. The greatest modifications are required when the torso is hidden with only the character's limbs or head exposed. In this case holes large enough for the head, arms, and legs to fit through are cut.

Another table is the variety used to chain or shackle torture victims to. Since this is often displayed in the upright position, it doesn't require legs. A large 8'x4' sheet of 1" plywood or pressed particle wood board painted dark brown or black works best. You can then add attachments like chains, wide leather straps, or shackles. Shackles are made from silver painted 3"-4" PVC pipe that is cut in half using hinges and padlock loop clips that are available from any hardware store.

Shackles made from 3" cut and hinged PVC pipe

Back view

Front view

A final variety of tables are the type that could be used by mediums or for seances, a simple card table, or an inexpensive round particle board table. Cover with a dark colored or unusually patterned cloth. If you borrow a table, and plan to cut a big hole in it for a trick, make sure to return it with a different tablecloth without the hole left on top.

DEVICES OF TORTURE AND PUNISHMENT:

We aren't going to have the space here to give you a history lesson on the names and purpose for each device, simply reproduce those in the drawing that you feel will fit in, or do a little research on the web for additional descriptions.

On occasion you can find an electric chair at a state auction, when they're upgrading to a solar powered model. Storage may pose a problem, so again, be creative with what to use this thing for year round, or construct it so the prop can be disassembled to be stored.

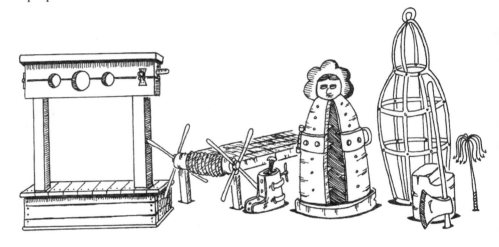

A walk through building materials, craft supplies, or hardware store will expose you to all the materials that can be used then painted to reproduce carbon copies. Remember, these things don't need to actually work, unless you have one of those pesky neighbors who routinely cuts his lawn at 8:30 am every Sunday morning.

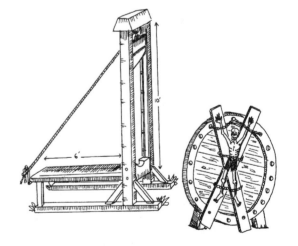

- ☠ **The Stockades:** These can be made out of wood, or any other building material that you have **available** which can be cut to size and assembled.

- ☠ **Beheading Block**: This one is easy. Just use a small round wastepaper basket used for rubbish (I've always **loved** that word), and paint the sides flat black, or flat brown with gray streaks to look like a section of tree trunk.

- ☠ **Guillotine**: This one is going to be a little more of an investment. We've provided a drawing as a guide, but be sure to construct the blade holder to allow the cardboard painted blade to retract back up into the holder. Also, install the blade holder stop to prevent the blade holder from falling down to the neck-hole, Be sure never to use it with a live person's neck at risk. Though it has been designed for safety, follow our suggestion of using a character in a hidden head **costume** and prop head, or a dummy with detachable head.

- ☠ **Electric Chair**: We hope you've paid up your electric bill on this **one**. If you use this we recommend some good sound effects and either a strobe, or make the lights blink on and off or dim in the room when it's turned on. The professional prop model sells for over $5,000.

- ☠ **Pendulum**: Either rig with electro-magnetic motor from home electronics store, or have hidden assistant help keep blade swinging. DON'T use a real blade.

- ☠ **Prison Cell**: This one takes up a lot of space for storage, so make it easily storable by connecting the four walls with door hinges. This allow for the removal of the hinge pins so the four walls can be stored laying flat.

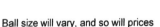

NOOSE INSTRUCTIONS

- ☠ **Hangman's Noose**: If you were a scout, this should be a snap to follow the drawing. Just don't tie up too much time learning it. Remember never tie one of these nooses around a live person's neck.

- ☠ **The Rack**: Don't let this one "outstretch" your budget, follow the simple drawing above, using on old wooden table and the cheapest building supplies available.

JACK-O-LANTERN:

Try a jack-o-lantern carving kit with elaborate designs. The patterns take a long time to poke out, but the results are great. There is also a wide selection of polyfoam jack-o-lantern, with choice of size, expression, color, internal lighting, and even sound effects. For added effect hide a speaker in the Jack-o-lantern, and surprise the treaters that take more than their share of treats.

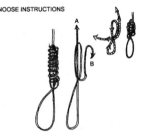

Jack-o-lantern

You could also decorate your own head as a jack-o-lantern using a make-up kit or mask, and stick your head through a hole in the table. Or stick your hand in through the hole inside the pumpkin to set off a camera strobe flash and simultaneously scream.

At least be sure to carve a jack-o-lantern to have out for the kids. Who would want to miss that fun tradition of scooping out pumpkin guts and saving the seeds to plant next spring (which Mom always throws out the next day)?

CRYSTAL BALL:

To purchase these things can get expensive, ($25-$300). Consider using one of the electrostatic plasma balls ($40-$90), or try a large glass globe replacement for a light fixture (larger building supply store's lighting department) clear or frosted. For a base use either a dark cloth wrapped around the bottom, or make one of wood. Use lights and dry ice for effects inside the globe.

Ball size will vary, and so will prices

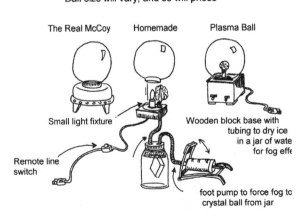

The Real McCoy   Homemade   Plasma Ball

Small light fixture

Remote line switch

Wooden block base with tubing to dry ice in a jar of wate for fog effe

foot pump to force fog to crystal ball from jar

3 TYPES OF CRYSTAL BALLS

GHOSTS:

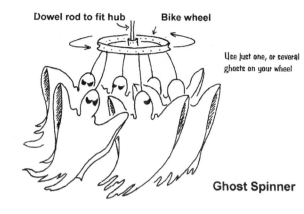

Dowel rod to fit hub   Bike wheel

Use just one, or several ghosts on your wheel

Ghost Spinner

There is a broad choice here. Try to use light weight white fabric (like a cheese cloth), so if you plan to use a hidden fan or hair dryer blowing up from underneath, its' flow gives good movement. Hang the fabric from the ceiling using heavy duty black thread. Consider spot lighting from below with a small bulb shielding the beam to only shine on the ghost. Try using overhead UV lights (24"-36" tube type only). Using a helium balloon underneath can add buoyancy, and attach control threads on opposite sides for lateral movement from helpers.

Another technique is to attaching the three overhead support lines (head and both hands) to a board mounted on an axial for motion. Also try using a lightweight wheel, like a 26" bicycle rim, with the lines tied to the side to give the effect that the ghost is floating in circles. Be sure to mount the wheel to an axial mounted high enough that it cannot be seen, paint wheel or board flat black. If you decide to use the starched and shaped cheese cloth trick, think of hanging a small AAA battery Krypton bulb flashlight from the inside at the base of the ghost with the beam shining up into the ghost. You can also project ghosts onto walls with silhouettes cut through the bottom of a shoebox. The sides of the box allow the light to project only through the image holes, creating crisp ghost figures. For best results, keep ghost projections moving around the room. You can also use shadow wheels or other silhouette devices.

DRIVE OR FLY UP WINDOW

Large Appliance Box

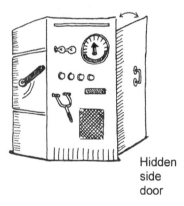

Hidden side door

Pop-up skull in chest

LABORATORY TRANSFORMATION BOX:

This is a full sized box large enough for a man to stand in, and is made up to look like something found in a laboratory. A refrigerator box obtained from a local appliance store is the cheapest way to go on this. Paint it flat black or silver, make several lever switches out of wood, and mount on front or sides. Use a string of low watt all clear or red Christmas lights around the outside, and buy several inexpensive fixture sockets on cords that support a 25 watt orange, red, or blue bulb, either the large Christmas light variety, or the standard bulb. Also, paint in fluorescent colors a variety of knobs to attach, anything else like needle meters, or whatever else you can get your hands on. Look at the home electronics store.

SKELETON SPRING BOARD:

This prop works best using a light weight latex skull that can be purchased for $10-$30, or even better, use one of the half torso corpse props from Death Studios $55-$70. Follow the instructions in the drawing. Attach to the backside of a door with a small bared window, or a wall with a window panel, or on a dumb waiter door.

SCARECROW:

This one is pretty basic, using 2"x2" boards as the cross wood supports. Consider effects like lighted eyes, a speaker in the head that you can talk through from a hidden location. Use as a decoy when you dress up to look like a poorly made scarecrow, waiting in an awkward pose or in a chair, to jump up at just the right moment. This works best when there are several other dummy scarecrows around, so they don't know which of you is real.

TRUNK:

This prop would be better to buy at a garage sale, flea market, church bazaar, or a junk dealer. You can even buy a cheap one from an import store. Paint it up to look aged and dusty. Then, consider mounting a half torso corpse prop on a springboard, with a trigger system designed to go off when the lid is opened. Try to vent a dryer duct pipe in from an unexposed side or bottom, then have a helper in another room scream like they are trapped inside the trunk. If you need to take out a big mouth, put a live badger in one, and challenge him to open it to release a spooky ghost…just kidding.

WITCH'S CALDRON:

This is one that would be hard to build yourself, unless you did so by making a two dimensional cut out from a 1" sheet of wood or piece of heavy cardboard, painting it black, and position it in front of a large plastic tub of water and dry ice. Otherwise, look around at import stores, discount department stores, or inexpensive kitchen supply stores. If you buy a large one from a Halloween prop or Costume store it may be expensive. You could also paint a half of a whisky barrel (sold for yard plantings) flat black, optional, make feet out of decorative fence post tops from a home building supply store.

CLOSING:

If you need ideas for lighting, pyrotechnics, or other electronic spark surprises you must visit the web site http://www.theatrefx.com/ (see the reference chapter)

We realize that most of these professional props are well beyond the budget of most of our readers. Our intention to include them was to show you how elaborate Halloween attractions have become.

There are hundreds of other props that were not included, but we'll save some of those for volume two. We hope that we've showed you where to find your raw materials to allow you to make some of your own props. With a little experience in prop building, you'll never throw anything away again, because you'll think of a use for it.

You may also develop the imagination and handiness to become a top-notch fix-it person. Good luck prop hunting, it'll be a lot of fun.

If you want to really see all this stuff in the comfort of your own home, read our reference chapter, then go surf the web. You'll be amazed at what you'll find. It's the absolute easiest way to browse the prop selection for ideas. Web sites often move, so if a listing is no longer valid, use the company name in a key word search with the top three search engines.

SPECIAL LIGHTING AND SOUND EFFECTS

How you light your layout or party has a dramatic effect on emotions. The sound then builds on this emotion to put your victims…or rather visitors, on edge. These are critical elements for creating surprise or fright. The older horror movies relied heavily on these two elements before the introduction of special effects or bloody gore. The tricks or visual effects you set will create a magnified reaction under the proper lighting and sound effects, so be sure to include this chapter as a key ingredient in your recipe for bedlam on Halloween night.

LIGHTING:

Throughout this section we will provide a broad collection of lighting tips, and describe the effect they're designed to create. Regardless, you must always individually experiment with your own unique display since so many conditions can effect the final appearance.

The first basic principle is that any direct lighting should still be kept low. This can be achieved by using low watt, colored bulbs, dimmer switches, light screens, and UV "Black" lighting.

BRIGHT LIGHTING

The only areas that you should expose to direct lighting are those decorated with high quality detailed props that can withstand the scrutiny of a prolonged stare. This can be very effective with well-costumed characters participating in the scene. Also when trying to display a well engineered trick or illusion additional light may be needed for the audience to discern what they are looking at. When focus is to be narrowed to a specific area, prop, illusion, or character, use mini spot lighting, which can focus a 4" beam of light on the subject. These can be controlled to flash on for just a few seconds for a different effect.

STROBE LIGHTING

The second type of lighting you can use is the multiple action strobe. This type of choppy flashing light is usually bright enough for the audience to see some detail in the scene, so again the props and characters must be of a higher quality and detail to master the reaction that you're seeking. Strobe lighting creates the illusion of motion, increased action speed, and confusion, making it ideal for a scene that erupts into a surprise action (like an escaped monster). It can also be effective to promote the illusion of motion from inanimate objects or props (like bats or ghosts hanging from a ceiling). The challenge with using a strobe is keeping other unwanted light out, which spoils the strobing effect. Be sure to test the strobe for proper brightness. Vendors are listed in the reference chapter that sell a full line of these strobes ranging $28-$100.

FLASHES

A third type of lighting is a single action strobe or flash. This is especially effective at creating disorientation and confusion. An example is to have a hallway with a costumed figure walking toward the group, hit it with a bright flash, then with eyes unadjusted to the dark, the group can only guess what it was they just saw and more importantly, where is it going. This is also effective to be used on a good prop in a dark room, was it real? Try positioning the strobe in different locations in the area, including behind the prop or character. Combine this with the use of multiple single flashes timed irregularly with enough time to allow the character to disappear to another position. You can buy floor mat switches that could be used to help trigger a surprise flash without tying up a helper.

BLACK LIGHTS

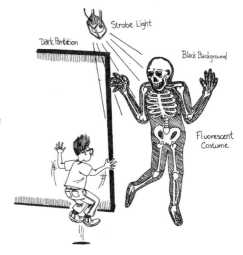

A fourth type of lighting is the UV or black light. This light only illuminates certain colors or materials, which helps in masking parts of your display that you don't want your audience to see. UV lighting is particularly sensitive to fluorescent and luminous paints. This type of lighting is a must for many of the scenes and tricks discussed in this book. It is important to have lights that are powerful enough to generate this effect.

Avoid the standard bulb-shaped UV lights. These tend to generate a lot of heat, but not very much light. Stick to the tube type. In most cases it is good to experiment, but two fixtures is more the norm. GE has a great 25" portable tube light that sells for between $22-$25 each.

The effect is improved when you can hide the bulbs from the audience's view, like attaching it to an inside wall not visible from the group's position. When a painted object is suspended against a dark non-reflective background, it appears to float. Test the area's existing light reflections before investing in black plastic sheeting or paint to darken the background. The colors even take on a dimension, with the lighter colors (yellows, oranges) appearing to be closer than those darker (blues, greens). By using less paint or even wiping off some, a faint glow can be achieved.

Also, creative things can be done with certain reflective fishing line that can be strung around a room with a figure behind it, then turn on the UV light after the audience has seen the back lit creature like it is now being contained with a laser beam cage. Further, certain materials are highly reflective under UV light (like select spider webbing fibers), experiment a little. Luminous powder can be mixed with make-up for a glowing effect.

COLORED LIGHT BULBS

A fifth type of lighting uses colored bulbs or screens (like those used in the theater). The blue colors create suspense and mystique, reds and oranges generate anxiety and fear, and green with a fog can be very eerie. Test out a few, but don't get too bright or there goes the atmosphere. Try keeping the spot lighting at floor level to create a spooky ground glow, especially when using a fog machine or dry ice. Control brightness with dimmer switches, try fading in and mixing different colors.

PROJECTION LIGHTING

A sixth type of lighting is projection lighting. This is used to light-specific figures, while leaving the remaining areas unlit. This can be done using several different techniques. The most popular involves silhouetting. This is where the desired shape is cut into an opaque surface like poster board, and is lit from behind to project a large shape of light. The back lighting requires shading (like being

boxed in) to prevent unwanted light to disrupt the effect. You can also perform the reverse of this where the area is lit and

the shape is cut out with the positive shape held up to the light (usually mounted on a thin stick) casting an enlarged shadow of that shape. Try this using UV light on a background that only a pattern on the wall reflects the light. It creates eerie shadows, or you can have a false wall made of paper or cloth, and position costumed characters or props behind it, then turn on a bright back light from behind the figures to cast their shadows onto what originally looked like a solid wall.

INDIRECT LIGHTING

A final type of lighting is called reflective or indirect lighting. Bouncing light off another surface (like a wall, floor, or ceiling) onto the object creates this lighting. This technique is used when

you only want the audience to see enough of an object or creature to distinguish its shape. From this shadow they can only assume what the object is based on the silhouette it casts. (Like a figure, a large spider, or bat) This illusion can save you big bucks on props when it's too expensive to buy the realistic looking variety. Indirect lighting is also effective in casting shadows in corners, closets, behind props, or anywhere else you plan to hide some surprise for your guests.

EFFECTS:

NIGHT SKY

Try painting a night sky scene. There are two ways. First, you can use luminous paint. Make dots of various sizes, with the larger ones even shadowed to create the natural lighting effect scene on the moon or other planets. Have a bright light positioned to illuminate the area to be turned on for about 15 seconds every 10-15 minutes when there are no spectators in the room. This recharges the luminescence in the paint. This can also be done using UV lighting, but test the background to assure nothing other than the paint glows. The advantage here is that you can test a variety of colors and shadowing, remembering the effect the color has on distance perception.

Second, a night scene can also be created by making holes of various sizes on a material dense enough not to allow the bright light that is projected from the opposite side to shine through anywhere other than the small holes. Have a helper use a laser pointer from a hidden position to cast a shooting star across the otherwise still scene.

INVISIBLE GHOUL

Another effect that requires just the right UV lighting is to have a character costumed in all black with the exception of white gloves, or painted with fluorescent or luminescent paint. Have them stand against a dark wall or corner with eyes and mouth closed and hands hidden under folded arms. They may also need to put some dark facial make up (test first) to be totally invisible. When the victim gets close the character opens eyes and mouth, and reaches out with white-gloved hands. Use white vampire teeth (Scarecrow®) and have the person scream for addition scares. Be careful not to touch anyone, someone is liable to take a swing at you.

MORPHING MIRROR ILLUSION

Consider using a 2 way 18" x 24" mirror framed on a wall. Tell the guests not to stare at their reflection too long, because it may conjure up the house's original owner who

was shot by a thief 100 years ago tonight. Then have a character on the opposite side made up like a corpse with a

LOW LIGHT →
BEHIND MIRROR
ON DIMMER

← FIGURE BEHIND
MIRROR
(Black Background)

bullet hole in their forehead, or a skeleton. Gradually turn up a spotlight aimed on the figure behind the mirror shining upward from below the face. It creates a morphing effect when properly performed with practice.

SOUND:

Setting up your scenes without sound is like getting dressed without underwear (except for the drafts). Have you noticed how important sound and music are to the cinema. Can you imagine watching your favorite horror movies with only dialog?

Sound is important for a variety of reasons when trying to scare people.

- ☠ It can create an unstable emotional atmosphere,
- ☠ It covers other background sounds that could distract from the effect,
- ☠ It helps to keep patrons from talking to each other and creating a distraction. (Which in turn generates a feeling of isolation),
- ☠ It may create confusion and disorientation.

There are many subconscious reactions to both sound and music, effecting each person a little differently. As you add more sound effects, a person's mind attempts to track and decipher each one. This can occupy the mental faculties normally used to balance rational thought, which increases the level of confusion. Consider using several levels of sound to create the same type of dimensional layering that an artist uses to paint a picture.

RULES FOR THE WARY:

- ☠ Your budget will clearly determine the caliber of sound system you will use, but shop around for quality differences for the same prices.
- ☠ You can always try to borrow equipment. We highly recommend this approach, since you'll only need it for the day.
- ☠ Be certain to get proper training on how to use this equipment, never abuse the system by pushing volume levels beyond wattage limits, or adding too many speakers.
- ☠ Be protective and hide all wiring to avoid accidents. No eating or drinking around the equipment, and no eating garlic or onions before using the microphone.

WHAT TO GET?

We could write two books on sound equipment, but I'm afraid you'll have to do your own homework on this one. You do want to attempt to find equipment that allows you to talk and project your voice. Here are some techniques to arrange and level your sound effects.

WHAT TO DO WITH YOUR SOUNDS?

Sounds should be layered. The more elaborate systems should have background sounds, mid-level sounds, foreground sounds, and a narrator.

BACKGROUND SOUNDS:

Keep the background sound loud enough to prevent you from hearing any other surrounding natural sounds or people talking to one another. Lots of bass and low tones help to mask sound, but also create vibration that can add to the atmosphere of fear. This level of sound effects can either be a haunting ballad of music (organ music can offer a mysterious appeal), like that played in the Disney Haunted Mansion, or repeated background sounds of environmental sounds, like a thunderstorm, crickets, owls, odd night sounds, or anything that repeats itself incessantly.

Use larger speakers for this level, and have them positioned throughout the display. Consider using either a CD or cassette player that has the continuous play option for yard or party displays.

MID-LEVEL SOUNDS:

The mid-level sound effects would also be sounds that repeat themselves, but without the frequency. Possibly moans and groans, chains rattling, scratching, howling, etc. These may change over time, but must have a greater volume than the background sound, so as not to be drowned-out. Face speakers towards the trick-or-treaters.

FOREGROUND SOUNDS:

The foreground sounds are those used to create shock. They come suddenly, unexpectedly, and are much louder than the other two sounds, but not so loud as to possibly create hearing loss. Midrange and tweeter speakers work best here, though I've heard a strong cannon base boom that almost knocked this fat guy off his feet. Use an electronic keyboard hooked to an amplifier or a megaphone for these types of effects. In many cases you don't even need a system, the characters themselves scream.

NARRATOR:

With all this noise going on, we also recommend a narrator with a set of strong lungs or a megaphone. The narrator's speaker can be placed in a bush to give the effect of his or her voice coming from everywhere and nowhere at the same time.

Remember, with sounds, the louder the better. Just build the volume one layer at a time, so each new layer is louder than the last. Play with volume levels until you get just the right effect.

WHERE DO YOU GET SOUNDS?

When it comes to the variety of prerecorded sounds and music there are a great many choices. For background, check out the environmental section of you local record shop. For mid level sounds, check you local party store for Halloween tapes. These are usually pretty good. For foreground sounds, you can consider making your own recording on cassette, or set up a system to create the sound just as the little beggars are walking up to ask for candy. The fun you can have watching their reactions as you startle them with a deafening, blood-curdling scream is amazing. These type of sounds can be created by hooking up a kid's noisemaker (machine gun, scream box, alien sounds, etc.) to an amplifier and speaker. Just look at your local toy store or in catalogs like Brainstorms for this kind of thing. It will take a little experimentation and a trip to your local Radio Shack, but the effect is worth it.

DIGITAL SOUNDS:

There are many unusual sounds that can be produced with a good keyboard synthesizer, not to mention what you can do with sound editing equipment. You'll have to try these yourself to see how they work for you. Use a combination of short clips recorded from other tapes, CDs or records, make and record your own sound effects, record from TV or radio, or best-yet record sound bites downloaded from the World Wide Web.

There is an amazing collection of sounds and music on the Web. Many of these are just sound bites, but there are longer clips too. Try to perform your searches when convenient, then book mark the sites, later return to download at non-peak times. Use a variety of search key words and search engines. There are interesting software programs designed to distort WAV files, to create unusual sound effects using your computer, and then transferring them onto tape.

MAN-MADE SOUNDS:

Finally, consider these ideas for making good old manual sound effects. This may involve:

- ☠ pounding on walls.
- ☠ clanging bells.
- ☠ dragging heavy objects.
- ☠ moans and howling.
- ☠ dropping a board.
- ☠ siren whistles.
- ☠ dropping chains or heavy objects on overhead floors.
- ☠ honking compressed air horns.
- ☠ playing an instrument in a melancholy tune.
- ☠ slapping a wall or door right when someone is beside it.
- ☠ dropping a metal plate on a concrete floor.

SOUND ADVICE:

This experience with sound equipment may open up a whole new career for you. Just remember that it all started with this book!

In our reference chapter there are catalogs and web sites that contain a wide variety of lighting and sound equipment that can do everything from making thunder and lightning, to projecting a whisper into an unsuspecting guest's ear from a hidden source. In particular, there is one reference to a lighting wholesaler called "Theater Effects", that has a fantastic collection of pyrotechnics, lighting and other special effects so unique, that most people are unaware of them.

For scaring kids in your yard, you should be well equipped. For a haunted house, you'll just have to spend some additional research time investigating your options and yet stay within your budget. As always, we recommend that you talk with as many people experienced in haunted house sound and lighting systems as possible. Contact them on the web by contacting various sites advertising their haunted house. You'll certainly get a lot of sound advice, and will hopefully be a little "brighter" for your efforts.

SAFETY:

✋ Provide hearing protection (foam earplugs) for volunteers working in the house who are exposed to this noise for prolonged periods.

✋ Always have emergency self powered lighting that can be quickly activated in the event of an emergency.

✋ In a maze have non-reflective signs pointing the way out but invisible in dark lighting.

✋ Also consider using low watt red Christmas light strands to illuminate the baseboards of walkways that are otherwise totally dark. This can also be done with UV lighting and painted Bugs, eyes, skulls, etc., but the guest clothing may also glow.

✋ Be certain that there are no overhangs, corners, irregular floor surfaces or sharp edges that someone could get hurt on. Nothing dampens the fun more than an injury when playing pranks. All helpers should carry flashlights.

FLOATING IMAGES:

Here is a plan for a neat projection trick good for anything you can take a slide of. By projecting an image into a pair of rotating mirrors the image is reflected in motion. This gives the appearance of the image floating up from the floor, like you would imagine a ghost arising from his grave. The illusion can be of a skeleton arising from a grave, a ghost floating up, a witch flying across the room, a large human hand, flying insects or bats, or even a monster.

To create the illusion you'll need:

- ☠ A projector (either a standard slide projector, or if you can buy an inexpensive toy projector)
- ☠ A slowly rotating AC motor (6-10 RPM) like those used in cheap animated Christmas figures or grill's rotisserie unit
- ☠ 2 mirrors measuring about 5"x 7", mount one to each side of a 1" thick wooden block of wood or Styrofoam
- ☠ Build a small frame that allows the motor to rotate the mirrors

The drawing shows you how to fabricate the frame. It can be built in a variety ways, with the objective to support the mirrors mounted on opposite sides of the block, to be rotated by the motor.

The mirrors must rotate on an axis high enough off the surface for your projector to shine the image directly into it. The shaft of the motor can be used as the pivoting axis for one side of the block, with the opposite side supported by a small rod resting in a whole in the frame. The mirrors must be level to rotate smoothly.

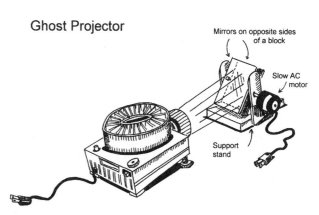

Ghost Projector

Mirrors on opposite sides of a block

Slow AC motor

Support stand

To create the slide of the image to be projected use slide film. Take the picture of the figure close enough to fill the frame. Use a black background, and be sure the object is well lit so it really stands out in the slide, or a white background and a shadowed figure. You can photograph a prop, a costumed assistant, or a cardboard cutout available at any party supply store. Just make sure it looks realistic enough, and has light, bright coloring. The prop can be of any size. Once completed, take this slide or slides, insert them into the projector and with the mirrors rotating, and project the figure into the room.

A video projected can also be used taping the figure using the same background guidelines.

Adjust and position the projection, and then position any supporting props like a tombstone or coffin. Get creative with this, use monster, ghosts, witches, a hand, or a head, even a picture of your mother-in-law.

IN CONCLUSION

We hope you're encouraged to experiment with ideas of your own. Lighting and sound can be used in so many different ways, that half the fun of setting up your haunt will be to play with the lighting and sound until you hit just the right combination. Even the simplest of layouts see dramatically improved effects when using them. Test everything you develop first before putting it into action. Good Luck.

SOMETIMES THINGS GO WRONG

Well, you've entered the home stretch in your quest to become a certified Haunt Master. I have included a photo of myself to satisfying that nagging question you've been asking yourself since reading the first page of this fine book, and that is, "Is this guy for real?" As you can see by the picture, I am not. I have been a cartoon all my life, and have adapted quite well to the unstable social environment of the 90s.

This chapter was written in an attempt to reduce common errors made by the "Novice Haunter". Though we hope everyone follows our instructions carefully before performing any of the tricks we have recommended, there's bound to be a few surprises or haunters who take things one step too far.

We were asked by the National Association of Trick-or-Treater's Survival (NATS) to help others avoid these terrible consequences. To date, we know of no one who has died as a result of these tricks, though Mr. Harold Sipps can now light a 75-watt light bulb in his mouth on a humid summer evening, and Sally Fourth can carve a full sized jack-o-lantern with only her teeth.

Read on, and you will learn, how on Halloween anything can happen. Realize that you can never be fully certified as a Haunt-master until you've also learned what NOT to do.

You may collect your diploma by faxing us your request.

If you wish to have your diploma notarized, officially allowing practice in multiple states, send a copy of your full name and return address along with a $100 processing fee to the publisher. He'll see to it that you're properly recognized for your decision.

OVER-INFLATED ROCKET

See that streak in the sky? Hear that whooshing sound? Who would have ever guessed it could fly so high? Though Stanley Plumpkin is well regulated himself, he seemed to have overlooked the regulator on the air tank. Inflating his 30 max PSI with over 200 PSI is something even NASA would not try. If you find something in your back yard resembling a 20' inflatable man (originally a 6' figure), please give Mr. Plumpkin a call at 666-SO-R-U.

INFLATABLE ARM:

It seemed like such a harmless prank, but Leonard didn't quite follow our instructions for positioning of the arm, and punched out little Lucy the witch. Now Dad is back to even the score. Poor Leonard, poor Lucy. I wonder if he listened to our recommendations on healthcare insurance?

CARRIED AWAY:

You've seen them at your kid's sporting events, you've seen them at parties, you've seen them at ball games, the guy who yells the loudest, brags the longest, knows the most, and generally takes things three steps too far. Stanley Hoksnoutis is one of those guys, and has taken a fun holiday like Halloween, and turned it into a nightmare for these poor trick-or-treaters by using something as sadistic as Math homework and twisting it into his holiday prank. And we wonder how our kids become so violent these days.

A DUMMY THREAT:

Doug never realized when setting up his dummy surprise layout that he would present a threat to humanity in the eyes of Superkid Sammy Hallenwacker. Yes, Sam decided that while taking the identity of his hero, Super Punk, he should also have the responsibility to rid the neighborhood of all potential menaces. To Sam, lifeless as they may seem, these dummies were definitely a danger to all trick-or-treaters. Maybe it was all the hand exercises from the video games, maybe it was from opening those new airtight freshness bags inside the kid's cereal boxes, but somehow this kid developed a strong grip. What a mess! Anyone know of a dummy repair service? Can anyone recognize which dummy was Doug?

20' AIRSHIP:

Look, in the sky, it's a bird, it's a plane, no…it's a 20' ghost. I guess Frank Fusstucker missed our recommendation about using the weights for windy conditions, and now…well if we could ask him, I'm sure he'd agree, "There's no place like home." Look at it this way Frank, you saved yourself the $75 for a hot air balloon ride, and such a clear and starry night too.

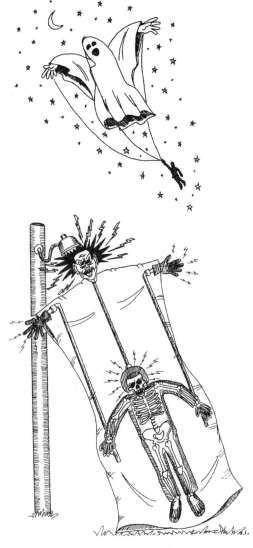

A SHOCKINGLY SCARY 10' GHOUL:

Mr. Sipps looked so spooky in that 10' growing ghoul outfit, but he looked down right frightening in it after bumping into that street light. He seemed to have an eerie glow to him. Silly Sipp, why did he use aluminum control poles instead of the recommended PCV? All that I can say is I'll bet the kids are getting a real "charge" out of the spectacle. How will he ever be able to spend those quarters that melted together in his pocket? How will he get the static cling out of his sheet? And how did he get that ghostly smoke to come out from under the sheet? That wasn't in our plans.

I guess we can all learn a lesson from Mr. Sipp, never leave chewing gum in your pants pocket when you put them in the laundry. Anyone wishing to send donations to help cover the Sipp's October electric bill may contact the publisher.

SHORT CIRCUIT:

Bob Pressley reports that the ever-popular vibrating mat does not increase vibrations with an increase in power, as witnessed by little Elmo after Bob's experiment with using 220 volt input resulted in humorous disappointment. Elmo is okay, but he says blackened tootsie rolls™ aren't at the top of his favorite candy list. Bob also continues his search for a product that can eliminate the smell of burnt latex.

Well, enough clowning around. You have to get to work if you ever plan to amount to a respectable haunter this Halloween. Be sure to use the resources listed in the following chapter, particularly the two major web sites. You may have to surf a little if these change and good luck.

THE TRICKY TALKING JACK-O-LANTERN:

The end of October can be a cold time of the year for a dousing, but tell that to "Ol' Man Foster". He decided that using water was cheaper than buying treats, and a lot more fun. Wait until he gets to meet little Toby's dad. He is use to playing in cold water after being a Navy Seal for 12 years. I bet Ol' Man Foster picks a new trick next year. One that he can control without the use of any of his limbs, since there's a good chance they will all be gone.

THE INVISIBLE MAN:

The floating shirt routine has been around for years, but the headless ironing man is new to me. How was Mr. Simpson to know that his playful idea of a scare would end up "flattened" by an imaginative trick-or-treater packing an iron? Maybe next year Mr. Simpson will read our book and step up to something using high voltage electricity or at least the air horn off a train.

FLOATING TRICK-OR-TREATERS:

As we have so often learned from the NASA space program, an invention can take on multiple applications based on the creativity of the user. In this case we see how the neighborhood trick-or-treaters have invented a "Ghost-go-round" out of Doug Ferguson's Fly Crank Ghost illusion. You can bet that once Doug realizes how his well engineered haunt has become the local thrill ride, he'll up the ante a little more next year by changing the 6 RPM motor to a variable speed high torque fan motor capable of over 200RPM. Once he triples the coverage of his home liability insurance he can see if he can put a trick-or-treater in space.

A TOUCH OF CRASS:

Granted haunting your yard may not be an activity which aspires to the same level of class as attending the ballet or a formal cocktail party, but those who resort to duct tape as the primary resource for repairs give home haunting a bad reputation. Here we have an example of how Mr. Canwider can't seem to find the time or materials to properly maintain the dead. Show a little respect Mr. Canwider!

ACTORS WITH A SENSE OF HUMOR:

Increasingly Trick-or-treaters and haunted attraction patrons are expressing their fear in aggressive forms of retaliation. This demands an increasingly more flexible sense of humor in your support actors. Give them a raise to 3 skulls an hour and all the change they can find.

AVOID CHEAP COSTUMES AND PROPS:

Sure, the kids of today have been desensitized from all the expensive high-tech special effects in today's age of multimedia entertainment, but common, you can spend a few bucks on the quality masks and props to avoid personal humiliation. You get enough of that at the office, why bring it home?

PERSONAL HYGIENE OF THE ACTORS:

No one likes to be told they have a hygiene problem, but in this case one of our key actors, the surprise greeter, BRUSHED THEIR TEETH before coming to haunt. Who ever heard of a decaying corpse with sweet breath? Maybe Edward here should be put on "Hurl Clean up" to help remind him how a real corpse should smell.

Enough for now. We hope you enjoyed the book and will look for the revised edition next Halloween.

PLACES TO SHOP & WHERE TO GET EVEN MORE SPOOKY IDEAS

Well, it looks like you're reaching the final pages before becoming certified to "Junior Level" Haunt Master. Now that you've read our efforts to totally distort your sense of humor, good judgment, and respect for children, we hope to share with you additional havens where you can dig even deeper into the graves of Halloween mischief.

This chapter first lists books and videos available on the subject, then lists the vendors who carry the supplies, props, and additional ideas and information to further your aspirations in Haunting.

All the following books and videos listed are available through BT Productions Terror by Design, the Chamber of Horrors, or the other vendors, also listed.

Due to the frequent changes of web site addresses, we have decided to only give you a few sites to browse. The remainder can be found with either key word browsing using words like haunted house props, Halloween, Halloween masks, body parts, ghosts, etc. If you don't have a computer, go to a university library, ask friends, some public libraries have links now, or break down and buy a computer with a good modem.

The two largest web site listed year-round are Haunted America at www.hauntedamerica.com and HauntWorld at www.hauntworld.com. These two have links to most major sites, shops, & haunts.

COSTUMES

BOOKS

COSTUME CONSTRUCTION BY KATHRINE HOLKEBOER
COSTUME DESIGN: TECHNIQUES OF MODERN MASTERS BY LYNN PECKTAL
CREATIVE COSTUMES FOR ANY OCCASION BY MARK WALKER
EASY-TO-MAKE COSTUMES BY KATHRYN HARRISON AND VALERIE KOHN

HAUNTED HOUSES

MAGAZINES

HAUNTED ATTRACTION Published Quarterly; @ PO Box 451 N. Myrtle Beach, SC 29597
Publication for the Dark Amusement Industry & home haunter $18.00 annually.

FRIGHT TIMES Published Quarterly; @ PO Box 4324, Shrewsbury, MA 01545
Publication for the Dark Amusement Industry & home haunter $18.00 annually.

HAPPY HALLOWEEN Published Quarterly; @ Global Halloween Alliance Corp. 1146 Wesley
Ave., Evanston, IL 60602-1163 Publication for the home haunter $18.00 annually.

UNDERGROUND ENTERTAINMENT, THE MAGAZINE Published Quarterly, @ PO Box 1113, Mt.
Juliet, TN 37121-1113 Publication for the Dark Amusement Industry & home haunter $18.00

BOOKS (ORDER ANY OF THESE BOOKS LISTED BELOW THROUGH BT PRODUCTIONS TERROR BY DESIGN)

BLACK ART BY L.L. IRELAND
BUILD YOUR OWN ILLUSIONS BY JIM SOMMERS
DARK ATTRACTION MANAGEMENT, MARKETING AND PROMOTIONAL TIPS BY JB CORN
DARK ATTRACTIONS ADVANCED DESIGNS BY JB CORN
FIELD OF SCREAMS BY MICHAEL M. CRUZ
HAUNTED HOUSE HALLOWEEN HANDBOOK BY JERRY CHEVEZ (VERY CREATIVE)
HAUNTED ILLUSIONS BY PAUL OSBORNE
HOW TO BUILD A HAUNTED HOUSE BY DARRON AND NEAL MCCARTER
HOW TO BUILD A PORTABLE MODULAR DARK ATTRACTION (A HAUNTED HOUSE) BY JB CORN.
HOW TO RUN A FINANCIALLY SUCCESSFUL HAUNTED HOUSE BY GHOST SHOW PERFORMER, TELEVISION
PERSONALITY AND MAGICIAN PHILIP MORRIS. (THIS BOOK IS THE GRAND DADDY OF THEM ALL)
SPECIAL EFFECT SOURCEBOOK BY ROBERT MCCARTHY
THE COMPLETE HAUNTED HOUSE BOOK BY TIM HARKLEROAD (HIGHLY RECOMMENDED)
THE DO IT YOURSELF HAUNTED HOUSE GUIDE BY MICHAEL TUCKER (A GREAT GUIDE)
THE HAUNTED HOUSE HANDBOOKS BY BAINES OF BAINES PRODUCTIONS

VIDEOS

GHOST MASTERS APPOX. 23 MINUTE
HAUNTWORLD THE MOVIE
HOW TO CREATE YOUR OWN HAUNTED HOUSE
PART I APPROX. 1 HOUR
PART II APPROX. 1 AND 1/2 HOURS
HOW TO DO FRIGHT RIGHT
HOW TO RUN A HAUNTED HOUSE
JB CORN'S VIDEO "HOW TO BUILD"
SECRETS OF THE HAUNTED MANSION
SPOOKY WORLD VIDEO 23 MINUTES LONG
HALLOWEEN ; THE HAPPY HAUNTING OF AMERICA

MAKE-UP HOW TO GUIDES:

BOOKS

GRANDE ILLUSIONS BY TOM SAVINI
GRAND ILLUSIONS BOOK II BY TOM SAVINI
MEN, MAKE-UP AND MONSTERS BY TONY TIMPONE WITH FORWARD BY CLIVE BARKER
MONSTER MAKEUP BOOK BY DICK SMITH
SPECIAL MAKE-UP EFFECTS
STAGE MAKEUP BY RICHARD CORSON
STAGE MAKE-UP BY RICH CORSON
TECHNIQUES OF THREE DIMENSIONAL MAKE-UP BY LEE BAYGAN
SPECIAL MAKE-UP EFFECTS BY VINCENT KEHOE

VIDEOS

BASIC FOAM MAKE-UP APPLIANCE
BEGINNERS GUIDE TO SPECIAL MAKE-UP EFFECTS VOL. 1., NO. 1 120 MINUTES
BOB KELLY ANIMAL FACES VIDEO
BOB KELLY CLOWN VIDEO
BOB KELLY'S INSTRUCTIONAL THEATRICAL MAKEUP DEVELOPMENT TECHNIQUES
CABLE CONTROLLED MECHANICAL MASK
DICK SMITH'S MONSTER MAKEUP VIDEO APPROX. 30 MINUTES
INTRODUCTION TO MAKE-UP EFFECTS
MBP PRESENTS THE ART OF SPECIAL MAKE-UP EFFECTS

INTRODUCTION TO MAKE-UP EFFECTS
BASIC FOAM RUBBER APPLIANCE
CABLE CONTROLLED MECHANICAL MASK
THE SECRETS OF DICK SMITH
VIDEO GUIDE TO SPECIAL MAKE-UP EFFECTS
TECHNIQUES OF LIFE CASTING
SCULPTING AND MOLDING A PROSTHETIC
FOAM LATEX & PROSTHETIC APPLICATION

MASKS:

BOOKS

MASK-MAKING HANDBOOK BY THURSTON JAMES
THE MASK MAKERS HANDBOOK BY ARNOLD GOLDMAN

VIDEOS

MASK MAKING THE DEATH STUDIOS WAY APPROX. 110 MINUTES
MONSTER MAKERS MASK MAKERS VIDEO APPROX. 60 MINUTES
PROFESSIONAL MASK MAKING VIDEO

MISCELLANEOUS HALLOWEEN STUFF:

BOOKS

THE ALIEN LIFE OF WAYNE BARLOWE BY WAYNE BARLOWE
GHOSTMASTERS BY MARK WALKER
GIGER'S ALIEN BY H.R. GIGER
SCARE TACTICS BY JOHN RUSSO
SPECIES DESIGN BY H.R. GIGER
SPOOKY MAGIC TRICKS BY DAVID KNOLES

VIDEOS

MAGIC OF THE SIDESHOW VIDEO 120 MINUTES
MARK WILSON'S VIDEO MAGIC COURSE VOL. 1
DOUG FERGUSON'S FLYING CRANK GHOST VIDEO

PARTIES & PROPS:

BOOKS

GREAT HALLOWEEN BOOK BY MARK WALKER
DR. LADY'S GUIDE TO MOVIE & TV MONSTER MASKS BY DAVID LADY
ENCYCLOPEDIA OF MONSTERS BY JEFF ROVIN
HOW TO BUILD A CORPSE BY DISTEFANO PRODUCTIONS
THE PROP BUILDER'S MOLDING & CASTING HANDBOOK BY THURSTON JAMES

CATALOG COMPANIES:

Cinema Secrets
4400 Riverside Dr.
Burbank, CA 91505
(818) 846-0579

The Anatomical Chart & Model Catalog
8221 Kimball
Skokie, IL 60076-2956
(800) 621-7500
http://www.anatomical.com

Death Studios
431 Pine Lake Ave.
La Porte, IN 46350
(219) 362-4321
http://www.monstermakers.com/death5.html

Intl. Magic & Fun Shop
16872 Hwy. 3
Webster, TX 77598
(281) 332-8142
http://www.fun-shop.com/

Halloween Productions, Inc.
1535 South 8th St.
St. Louis, MO 63104
(314) 241-3456
http://www.halloweenproductions.com/

Halloween Mart
5525 S. Valley View
Suite 7
Las Vegas, NV 89118
(800) 811-4877
www.accessnv.com/halloween/home.htm

DiStefano Productions
http://distefano.com/order.htm

Cutting Edge
1920 New Castle Ct.
Arlington, TX 76013
(817) 461-3514
http://www.screams.com

GAG Studios
11523 US 223
Blissfield, MI 49228
(517) 486-4055

The Monster Makers
7305 Detroit Ave.
Cleveland, OH 44102
(216) 657-7739
http://www.monstermakers.com/

The Chamber of Horrors
P.O. Box 2587
Brentwood, TN 37024-2587
(615) 252-6795
http://www.telalink.net/~chamber/

Scarecrow, Inc.
750 Farroll Rd. #E
Grover Beach, CA 93433
(805) 473-2562
http://www.webcom.com/verdun/

The Nightmare Factory
P.O. Box 1181
Dripping Springs, TX 78620 (512) 858-5063
http://www.nightmarefactory.com/

Theatre Effects
642 Fredrick St.,
Hagerstown, MD 21740
PO Box 957
Funkstown, MD 21734-0957
(301) 791-7646
http://www.theatrefx.com

Special Effect Supply
543 West 100 North #3
Bountiful, UT 84010
(801) 298-9762
http://www.xmission.com/~spl_efx/index.html

Doug Ferguson c/o Phantasmechanics
Box 209, 5000 W. Esplanade
Metairie, LA 70006
http://members.aol.com/barbferg11/fcgpre.html